Guitar *signature licks*

The Best of BLACK SABBATH

A Step-by-Step Breakdown of the Guitar Styles and Techniques of Tony Iommi
by TROY STETINA

Cover photo by Chris Walter/Photofeatures International

ISBN 0-7935-8790-5

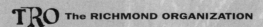
TRO The RICHMOND ORGANIZATION

DISTRIBUTED BY

HAL•LEONARD®
CORPORATION
7777 W. BLUEMOUND RD. P.O. BOX 13819 MILWAUKEE, WI 53213

Visit Hal Leonard Online at
www.halleonard.com

INTRODUCTION

Black Sabbath is the original "black metal" band, replete with horror-film themes and gothic imagery. They pushed music to previously uncharted levels of heaviness throughout the seventies, and set the stage for the hard-edged styles of 1980s thrash and death metal, as well as the heavier side of 1990s alternative rock. Their powerful influence upon countless guitarists throughout the world cannot be denied.

The story of Black Sabbath began in Birmingham, England in the late 1960s. The quartet—originally composed of vocalist John "Ozzy" Osbourne, guitarist Tony Iommi, bassist Terry "Geezer" Butler, and drummer Bill Ward— gained a fervent local following as a blues band called Earth. After learning that there was another band going by that name, however, the four renamed themselves, adopting the monicker Black Sabbath—the title of both an old horror movie starring Boris Karloff as well as that of a song the group had already composed. This name perfectly reflected the group's growing interest in supernatural and occult themes, which would come to dominate their lyrics and fuel the band's dark image and signature sound.

Their debut self-titled release, *Black Sabbath* (1970), initially attained only moderate success. It was their follow-up album later that same year, *Paranoid*, which first earned the band international acclaim with such classic metal masterpieces as "Iron Man," "War Pigs," and of course the title track, "Paranoid." After extensive touring in both Europe and the United States, a third release, *Master of Reality* (1971), cemented the band's growing popularity and commercial success. Also, on this landmark recording, the band began to experiment for the first time with ultra-low (C♯) tuning, to accompany their dark lyrical sorties with a deeper and darker tone. This would come to be a dominant and unique characteristic of the band's sound over the next number of years.

The group's creative powers were still in high gear as the fourth and fifth albums, *Black Sabbath Vol. 4* and *Sabbath Bloody Sabbath*, were released in 1972 and 1973, respectively. After five ground-breaking albums in just four short years, their status as the musical voice of the underworld was secured. Further efforts, including 1975's *Sabotage* continued to build upon their visionary art-rock tradition.

As with all important rock, it is as much a social commentary as a musical force, and Black Sabbath was no exception. Perhaps less obvious than their "evil" image, one finds upon closer inspection that the majority of lyrics invoke not evil messages at all, but simply social issues of the time as well as cryptic warnings. One common theme is to warn of the fate that will befall our evil ways, either as individuals ("Black Sabbath," "Paranoid") or as a world bent on nuclear destruction and hatred ("War Pigs," "Children of the Grave")—essentially as if the band were setting to music the biblical book of Revelation. Another theme is far-reaching science fiction and space travel ("Iron Man," "Into the Void") sometimes interlaced with mind travel via drug-induced, astral projection ("Supernaut"). The late sixties psychedelic drug culture morays were also explicitly set forth ("Sweet Leaf"). In many ways, the band's music was a backdrop reflecting society's ongoing dialog on priorities, right and wrong, good and evil, and where we are headed as a culture. Their focus on anti-war, ecology, and mind-expanding drug themes rode the forefront of controversy and continued to help push these 60s issues into the next decade.

Looking beyond the black-magic trappings, guitarist Tony Iommi is actually a fairly straight-ahead electric blues-rock player in the vein of Eric Clapton and Jimmy Page—in particular this is apparent when one examines his lead guitar style. However, it cannot be denied that his compositional finesse and distinctly heavier riffs are ultimately the items that help set his musical endeavors apart. In the years that followed, Tony would also be the glue that would keep Black Sabbath "on the map," churning out new material.

Vocalist Ozzy Osbourne left the band briefly in 1977 due to personal problems, but returned in 1978 to complete *Never Say Die* and perform on the subsequent tour. However, it was not to last, and he and the rest of the band parted ways in early 1979. Ozzy would go on to achieve even greater commercial success on his own solo career, initially teaming up with American guitarist Randy Rhoads. Meanwhile, Black Sabbath would forge ahead with former Rainbow vocalist Ronnie James Dio, adding two powerful new recordings to the Black Sabbath discography, *Heaven and Hell* (1980) and *Mob Rules* (1981).

After Dio eventually split to pursue a solo career of his own, Sabbath went through a long period of personnel changes—at times the only common denominator being Tony Iommi. But the recordings continued and the band remained a viable creative force. Now, nearly thirty years since they began, occasionally Ozzy and the original Black Sabbath members have been known to share the stage for some nostalgic moments and classic tunes.

The Songs

The songs on the accompanying audio CD include the following:

"Black Sabbath"—*Black Sabbath*
"N.I.B."—*Black Sabbath*
"Iron Man"—*Paranoid*
"Paranoid"—*Paranoid*
"War Pigs"—*Paranoid*
"Sweet Leaf"—*Master of Reality*
"Children of the Grave"—*Master of Reality*
"Into the Void"—*Master of Reality*
"Supernaut"—*Black Sabbath Vol. 4*
"Sabbath, Bloody Sabbath"—*Sabbath Bloody Sabbath*
"Symptoms of the Universe"—*Sabotage*
"Heaven and Hell"—*Heaven and Hell*

The Recording

Guitars and Bass:	Troy Stetina
Drums:	Brian Reidinger

Produced at Artist Underground, New Berlin, Wisconsin.

BLACK SABBATH

Words and Music by Frank Iommi, John Osbourne, William Ward, and Terence Butler

Figure 1 — Intro and Verse

Recorded in only two days for a reported 600 English pounds (at the time roughly equivalent to $800), Black Sabbath's self-titled debut album was released, appropriately enough, on Friday the 13th of February, 1970. The opening cut carried the band name and set the tone right from the start. Foreshadowing the epic art-rock styles that would come to fruition in the latter part of the decade, this dark opus is strongly evocative and displays a highly creative and unusual song structure.

The first half of the song is slow and brooding, dominated by the twisted sound of the *tritone* employed as a melodic interval (which simply means that the notes follow one another in sequence, as opposed to the notes of the interval sounding simultaneously, as a chord). Also known as a diminished fifth or augmented fourth, the tritone is the "evil interval." During the sixteenth century this musical outlaw was dubbed "diabolus in musica," literally, the devil in music; its turbulent, unsettled quality was seen as representing the seething pit of hell presumed to lay beneath mortal reality. With such a history, it comes as no great surprise that we find this interval playing a significant role in Black Sabbath's sound! In the wake of their pioneering musical innovation, many of today's heavier bands now commonly incorporate the tritone.

The opening riff first anchors the tonal center with a G5 power chord followed by the octave root, G, played as a single note. Be sure to release pressure on the lower notes of the G5 power chord so that they do not continue to ring under the single-note octave root, G. Then the tritone is invoked in stark simplicity with the melodic leap to C♯. Notice the unusual and disjointed leap provided by the tritone as a melodic interval. An alternating sequence of a trill between the ♯4th and 5th (C♯ and D) followed by a single ♯4th tone performed with finger vibrato creates a slightly varied articulation and sets up an ABAB form for the riff.

In preparation for the verse, the dynamic level drops, yet the tritone figure remains intact as a single-note phrase, bringing with it a sense of suspense and imminent peril lurking throughout. Roll your guitar's volume knob down to clean up the sound a bit in measure 9, and pick the strings more softly. Both the trill as well as finger vibrato articulations are abandoned.

3 **Featured Guitars:**
(right channel on audio)
Gtr. 1   meas.   1-28

4 **Slow Demos:**
Gtr. 1   meas.   1-4

Fig. 1

Figure 2 — Interlude, Guitar Solo, and Outro

As things "heat up" for our doomed protagonist portrayed in the lyrics, a faster, secondary riff emerges to mirror the rising level of desperation. The one-measure triplet-based motif spells out six of the seven notes found in the G natural minor scale (G-A-B♭-C-D-E♭-F), or Aeolian mode. Consistent alternate picking, beginning with a downstroke, is recommended. (This places upstrokes beginning on beats 2 and 4.)

A third distinct musical idea—an alternating sequence of G major to G minor seventh chords—enters as a setup for the guitar solo and continues underneath it (Gtr. 2). Over this foundation, the lead guitar (Gtr. 1) opens the solo in the familiar "box 1" or primary pattern of G minor pentatonic, located at the third fret, and builds incrementally. In particular, notice in measure 30 how Tony shifts up the fretboard via a series of unison string bends, arriving in the octave position of box 1, in measure 31. Here, comfortably established in fifteenth position, he hovers for the remainder of the solo, drawing on familiar rock lead guitar cliche patterns. These generally involve string bending of the 4th to the 5th (C to D), the minor 7th to the root (F to G), and the minor 3rd to the 4th (B♭ to C). Also notice the vibratoed quarter-tone bends on the minor 3rds in measures 42-43, pointing toward Iommi's strong blues influence. The outro section consists of simply an accented rhythmic variation of the same G-Gm7 chord sequence first seen leading into the guitar solo section.

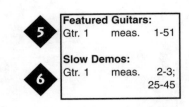
Fig. 2

Is it the ____ end ____ my _ friend? ____   Sa - tan's com - in' ____ 'round ____ the   bend. ____

Peo - ple   run - nin'   'cause ____ they're   scared. ____   You

peo - ple bet - ter ___ go ___ and ___ be - ware. ___ No, ___ no, ___ please, ___ no. ___

Guitar Solo

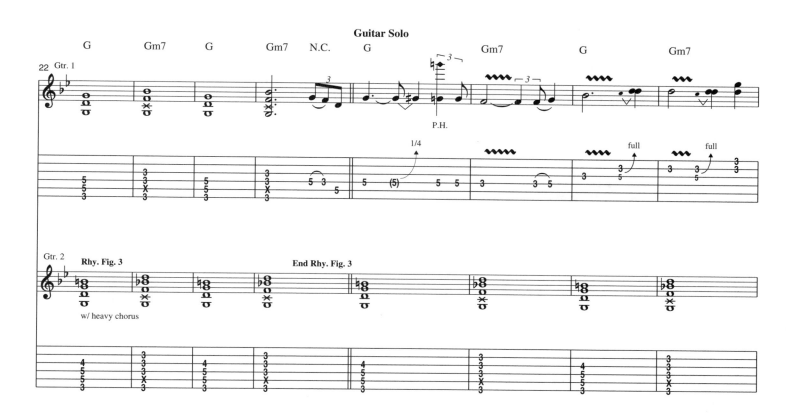

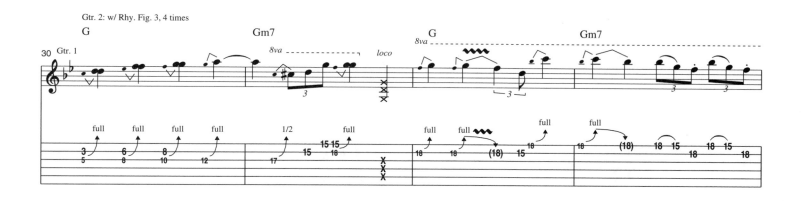

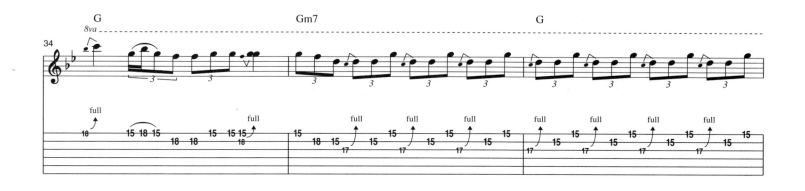

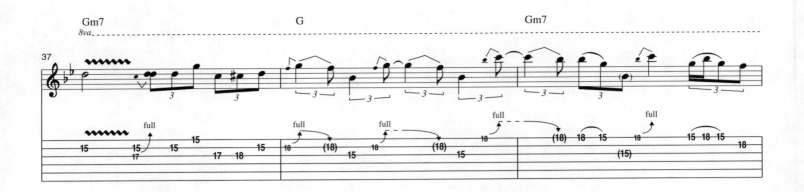

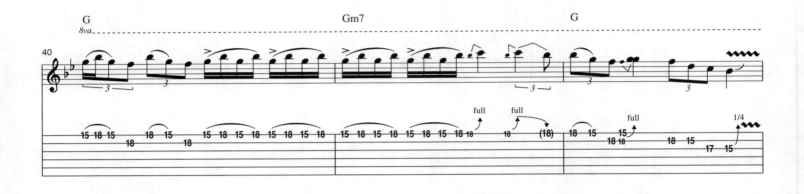

Outro
Gtr. 2: w/ Rhy. Fig. 3, 1st 2 meas.

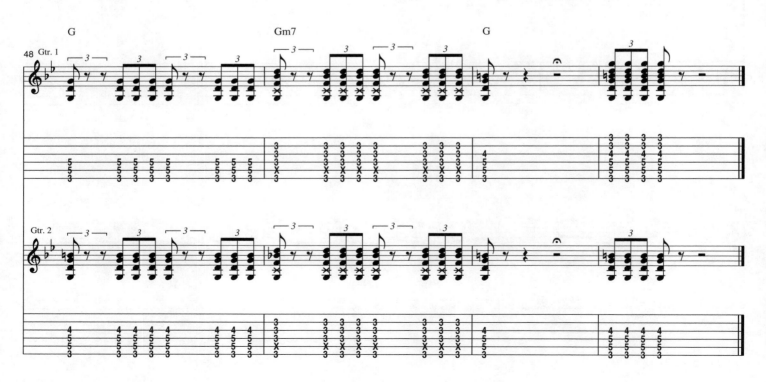

N.I.B.

Words and Music by Frank Iommi, Terence Butler, William Ward, and John Osbourne

Figure 3 — Intro, Verse, Interlude, Verse, and Bridge

Another standout track from the debut Sabbath album, "N.I.B." shows a more straightahead, hard-driving aspect of the band's style. Over the years, much speculation has emerged as to what the initials "N.I.B." actually stand for, the most common belief being "Nativity in Black." According to Iommi, however, the truth is much less profound. The real story is that the name came about as the result of an inside joke. Bill, the drummer, used to have a beard that came to a point, and one day Ozzy said that it looked like an "ink pen nib." After that remark, the other band members began referring to Bill as "Nib." Then, for some unknown reason, the track became dubbed with this name as well. To make it more cryptic, they put periods after each of the letters, suggesting some hidden meaning. The real message...just the guys kidding around!

The main riff is in power chord dyads rooted on the sixth string. These are played high on the neck which tends to give a deeper tone, an approach that Iommi often prefers. The riff employs E5, D5, G5, and F#5. Looking at the root movement, we can see this drawing upon the dark, haunting qualities of E natural minor (E-F#-G-A-B-C-D). Short fills grace the end of each two-measure phrase.

Another signature of the Black Sabbath sound can be found in the song structure itself. It is highly unusual by virtue of the fact that it completely omits the traditional chorus form, instead placing the main vocal hooks in the short, catchy melodies of the verse. This is then followed by an instrumental interlude rather than a chorus. You could also think of this interlude as acting like a kind of "instrumental chorus" in a sense.

Musically, the interlude section features an interesting interaction between guitar and bass in the form of *oblique motion*. The guitar holds a repeating, one-measure minor pentatonic figure, statically centered on E, while underneath, the bass moves down the E natural minor scale through the notes E-D-C (root, minor 7th, minor 6th). The phrase culminates on B, the V chord. The bridge then utilizes the same idea but in reverse. Here it is the guitar that moves down through the E-D-C pattern (each harmonized in 5ths, as power chords), while the bass holds an E. Again, both instruments join together on the final B chord (V chord).

Featured Guitars:
Gtr. 1   meas.   5-33

Slow Demos:
Gtr. 1   meas.   5-8;
                        17-20

Fig. 3

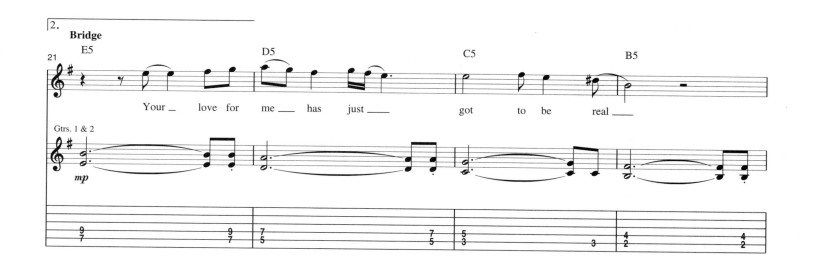

2.
Bridge

Your __ love for me __ has just ____ got to be real __

be - fore you know __ the way __ I'm go - in' to feel, __

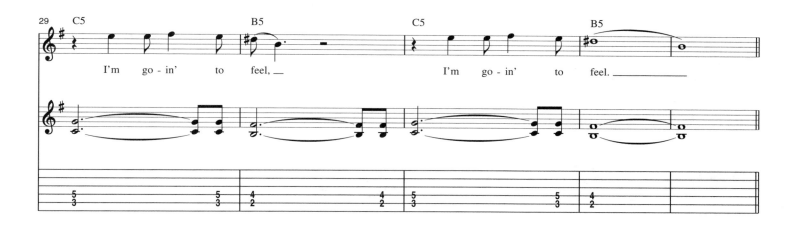

I'm go - in' to feel, __ I'm go - in' to feel. _____

Figure 4 — Guitar Solo

The first guitar solo, shown here, is an excellent example of Tony's early lead guitar approach. Tracked by two lead guitars, it is actually two different solos sounding simultaneously, at times playing in unison and at times veering apart from one another in an improvisational venture. Although both guitars are tracked on the accompanying audio, here we will concentrate on the featured (Gtr. 1) part.

The solo begins with a strong theme statement (measures 1-4) played in unison, which steps up the E natural minor scale (E-F#-G-A-B-C-D). Notice the interesting *rhythmic displacement* bracketed in measure 1, whereby the first beat and a half is repeated, with the second repetition beginning on the upbeat of beat 2—moving the notes so they occur against the beat exactly opposite from that of the first repetition.

In the next four measures (5-8), the two guitars veer apart from one another rhythmically as he builds with a loose, improvisational feel. This section utilizes the "box 4," or secondary box shape of the E minor pentatonic scale (E-G-A-B-D).

Following this brief excursion, he returns to the theme. Although somewhat altered in its second incarnation, it is still recognizable as being a recurrence of the original idea, and both guitars play in unison.

The final four measures (13-16) again feature improvised lines and, as the solo's climactic peak, are played in the higher register—the octave box 1 of E minor pentatonic located at twelfth position. Note the rhythmic displacement pattern of three notes repeated against a sixteenth-note rhythm in measure 13.

Featured Guitars:
9 Gtr. 1   meas.   1-16

Slow Demos:
10 Gtr. 1   meas.   1-16

Fig. 4

* Track 9 begins 4 meas. before Fig. 4

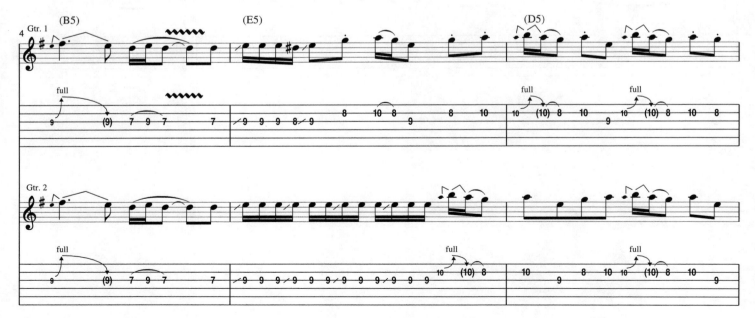

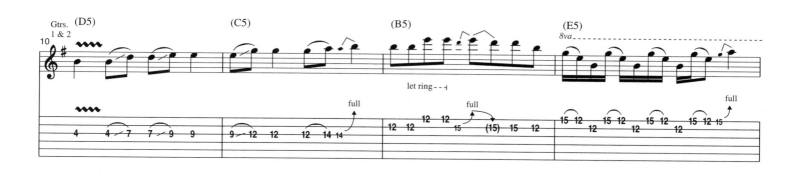

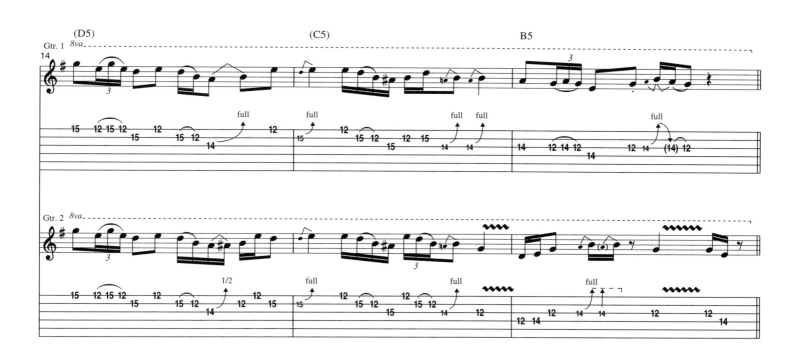

IRON MAN

Words and Music by Frank Iommi, John Osbourne, William Ward, and Terence Butler

Figure 5 — Intro, Verse, and Interlude

The band's second album, *Paranoid*, was released September 18th, 1970—just seven short months after their initial effort. It was this album, recorded in a mere five days, that truly launched the band toward stardom and cemented their position as the reigning masters of metal with such works as "Paranoid," "War Pigs," and the epic classic, "Iron Man."

"Iron Man" is a grand-scale, six-minute metal masterpiece containing at least ten distinctly different musical sections. Recounting a Sci-Fi self-fulfilling prophecy, the lyrics tell of a man who travels into the future where he witnesses the apocalypse. But when he returns to warn the world, nobody cares to heed his warning or help him. In revenge, then, he destroys mankind and finally it is clear that he himself is the cause of the apocalypse of which he foretold.

The tune opens with a single kick drum pulse, setting the stage upon which the plot will unfold. Gtrs. 1 & 2 enter with a bending-behind-the-nut technique. Press on the sixth string between the nut and the tuning machine (on the headstock) to bend the pitch up, then release down to an unbent E string. Or, if you have a locking vibrato system, simply pull up on the bar and then release it to the original position.

The immortal riff enters next, played horizontally on the neck in all power chords, rooted on the sixth string. The opening B5 seems to act like a temporary tonal center, but juxtaposed against the E foundation previously established, B5 actually produces the tense, unstable quality of holding the V chord here and throughout the bulk of the song. Over its E tonal center, the notes B, D, E, F♯, and G (5th, minor 7th, root, 2nd, and minor 3rd) once again draw upon E natural minor (Aeolian mode).

Full power chords give way to a single-note, "stepped-down" version of the riff in the verse, with vocal melody in tow. Here the position also shifts to accommodate the notes on thinner strings, thereby adding a tonal contrast to the texture contrast. We also see the "chorus-less" structure emerge. Verses appear broken in half with the power chord riff sandwiched in between. This is followed by an instrumental interlude. Still dominated by the V chord feel, the interlude points strongly toward E as being the real tonal center, particularly in measure 20. Note the chromatic passing tone of B♭ used between A and B, as well as the G♯ note which temporarily hints at E major.

Featured Guitars:		
11	Gtr. 1	meas. 3-28
Slow Demos:		
12	Gtr. 1	meas. 9-10; 13-14

Fig. 5

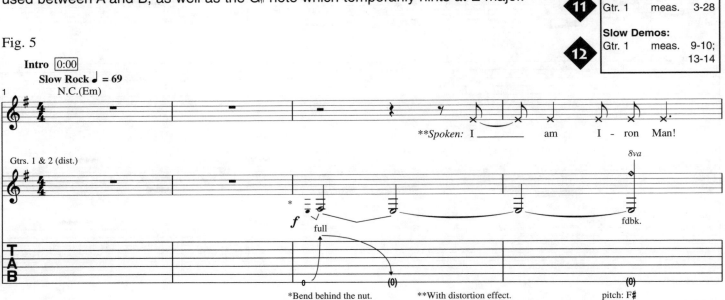

*Bend behind the nut.   **With distortion effect.   pitch: F♯

Figure 6 — Bridge, Interlude, Guitar Solo, Interlude

This section demonstrates the widening compositional scope of the band, functioning almost as a mini-composition within the larger arrangement. Incorporating modulation as well as several new riff elements, the interlude section acts as both intro and outro to the guitar solo.

The bridge opens on the tonic chord (E5) and features a pentatonic-styled E5-D5-Bm (i-♭VII-v) progression. On B, a new riff is introduced, climbing up the B blues scale (B-D-E-E♯-F♯-A) with an added chromatic passing tone of A (major 7th). Next, a new interlude section then modulates up to C♯ and descends the C♯ minor pentatonic scale with a highly syncopated rhythm in double time (twice as fast).

The solo section itself is an improvisational flurry—not only on the guitar, but also on the bass. This is at sharp contrast to the highly complex compositional nature of the tune, and provides a welcome relief, as well as allowing both musicians to stretch out and cut loose a bit.

Perhaps the most striking signature feature of this solo is Iommi's penchant for almost continuous phrasing. Unlike most rock soloists who phrase in distinct sections of two- or four-measure licks, Tony deliberately runs across these imaginary phrase "boundaries" and blurs the solo almost into one long, run-together phrase. This has the effect of creating an almost psychedelic or "free-jazz" feel within the hard rock context. Yet, at the same time, the solo does manage to move steadily through several different stages.

It kicks off in the lower to mid register. Measures 13-16 center on C♯ minor pentatonic box 4, with its added low extension. Note the repeated motif in measure 15, which resolves into the start of measure 16 and pauses. Then, in the middle of that measure, he shifts abruptly into box 1 (ninth position) for a barrage of pickup notes into measure 17. This is about as close as he gets to typically distinct phrasing.

In measure 17, he hammers on the major 3rd (E♯) in an otherwise minor pentatonic lick, a traditional blues approach of mixing major and minor freely. Measures 20-21 are the peak, or climax, of the solo, after which he meanders down through C♯ minor pentatonic box 1, arriving at last on the tonic note, or root, C♯. Measures 25-28 feature grace note hammer-ons to C♯ from B (minor 7th) in a rhythm that has become a metal/hard rock staple. This wraps up the solo nicely and acts as a cue for the band, setting up a transition pivot into the following interlude as a solo outro. Finally, the band modulates back down a whole step to the original key utilizing the B blues riff first seen as part of the bridge.

This entire section, then, can be viewed as a kind of form *ABCBA*...in other words, it moves systematically (sections "A" and "B") up to the solo as a peak compositional point (section "C") then it steps back in reverse order to once again arrive at the starting point.

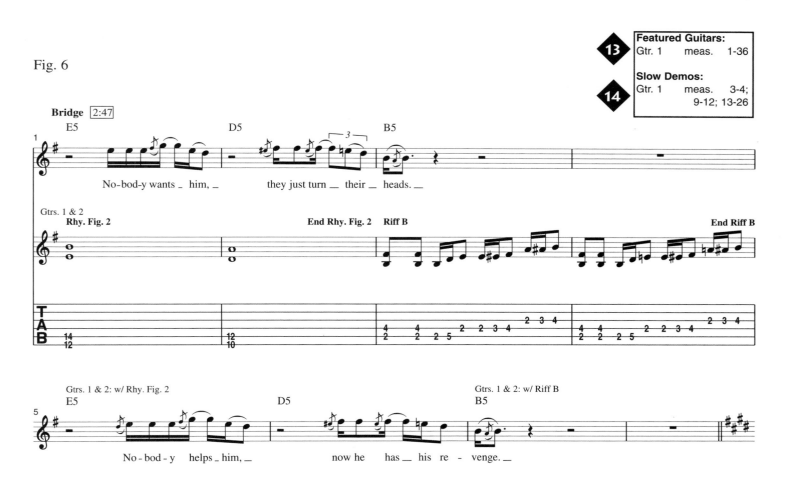

Fig. 6

Featured Guitars:
13 Gtr. 1   meas.   1-36

Slow Demos:
14 Gtr. 1   meas.   3-4;
            9-12; 13-26

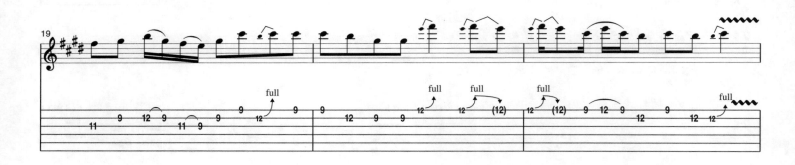

Figure 7 — Interlude, Intro Reprise, Guitar Solo, and Outro

Following the final (fifth) verse, the original instrumental interlude enters once again, but with a different ending—this time it lingers on an A note, under which the drums set up a double time groove that rides out to the end of the song. Over this quickening pace, the guitars briefly recap the original behind-the-neck bending scenario with the ringing low E string, then launch into a new musical section firmly planted in the key of E minor.

The bass guitar moves down through the sequence E-D-C♯-C, mixing E Dorian (E-F♯-G-A-B-C♯-D) and E natural minor (E-F♯-G-A-B-C-D) tonalities. Over this, the guitar plays a slightly embellished harmony line. In measures 17-18, the guitar part simply moves in parallel with the bass. But in measure 19, as the bass moves down to C♯, the guitar moves up in contrary motion, returning to E—which in this instance functions as C♯'s minor 3rd. A series of quarter-note triplets caps off the end of each two-measure phrase.

Notice the eighth-note triplet figure nestled within the second quarter-note triplet (measure 20). Since the second and third notes of that eighth-note triplet are played as a hammer and pull, you should only pick six times total in measure 20—once on each of the six quarter-note triplet subdivisions. (The first note of the eighth triplet is actually the fifth quarter-note triplet of the measure.)

A brief guitar solo erupts in measures 21-32. Utilizing two separate guitar tracks (Gtrs. 1 & 2), this is really two solos in one with both parts overlapping in improvised madness. Focusing on Gtr. 1, it begins in the low extension of box 4, E minor pentatonic (E-G-A-B-D), then promptly shifts up into box 4 "proper." Note the prominent 1 1/2 step bends from the root (E) up to the minor 3rd (G) on the third string in measures 21-22. This is a favorite Iommi bending position.

In measure 25, Iommi shifts higher yet, into the upper extension of box 4 (or, box 5) of E minor pentatonic and employs a Hendrix-inspired bending idea, pushing the root (E) up a whole step to the 2nd (F♯) and temporarily drawing upon that diatonic tone in a pentatonic context. More motivic 1 1/2 step "overbending" appears in measures 29 and 30 as the solo winds down toward its close.

Finally, guitars sink down to join the bass in the original harmony phrase that presaged the guitar solo. The outro consists of three repetitions plus the final three ending accents.

Fig. 7

Featured Guitars:
Gtr. 1   meas.   1-45

Slow Demos:
Gtr. 1   meas. 17-20;
                    21-32

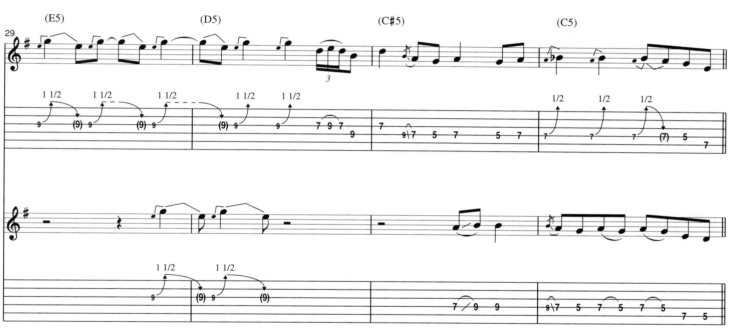

Outro

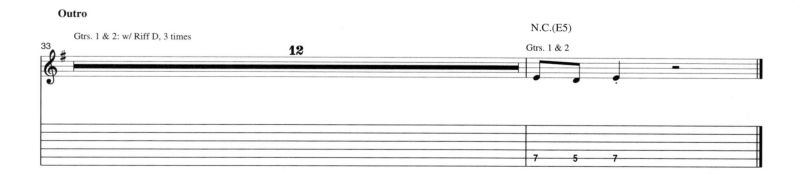

PARANOID

Words and Music by Frank Iommi, John Osbourne, William Ward, and Terence Butler

Figure 8 — Intro, Verse, Interlude, Verse, Bridge

Exploring the subject matter of a mentally disturbed man sinking ever further into depression and paranoia, "Paranoid" proved a perfect vehicle for Sabbath's darkly expressionistic, high-energy style. As both the album's title track and single release, the song helped propel *Paranoid* to capture the #1 position on the U.K. charts as well as a respectable showing of #12 in the United States, reinforced by successful and grueling tours on both sides of the Atlantic.

Several aspects of the band's maturing style can be found in this landmark tune. The driving palm-muting technique welded to hard-rocking riffs—which would become a heavy metal staple—was practically invented by Sabbath. This palm mute technique dominates the verse riff of "Paranoid." Lay the heel of your picking hand lightly over the ends of the strings where they meet the bridge saddles. Now when you pick, the strings will produce a muffled, percussive and "bassier" tone which, when the distortion is cranked up, becomes a thick "crunch" with driving low end. For the accents at the end of each two-measure phrase, lift off the strings and allow the chords to ring out strongly—although the final chord is to be cut off abruptly, as *staccato* is indicated. Use both the fret hand and the picking hand to stop the strings from ringing after this sharp chord jab.

Also, notice once again the unique Black Sabbath arrangement approach of entirely omitting the chorus structure. The vocal hooks appear as a series of compact verse melodies, between which, short instrumental interludes act to replace the traditional chorus form. This has the effect of producing a tighter, fast-moving tune, with far more than the usual number of verses. ("Paranoid" has five verses in a very short, 2:45 tune.) Short sections such as these also allow for a wider variety of possible arrangement scenarios—a flexibility which Sabbath exploited to great effect, creating unpredictable song forms which still inspire countless guitarists to this day.

	Featured Guitars:
17	Gtr. 1 meas. 1-36
	Slow Demos:
18	Gtr. 1 meas. 1-2; 5-8

Fig. 8

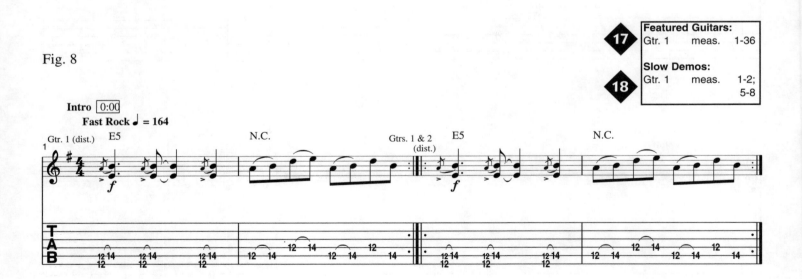

Figure 9 — Guitar Solo

The solo to "Paranoid" is a classic. It consists of a single guitar played through an octave pedal, which adds a note one octave lower than what is played. This can be heard on the album as well as on the accompanying audio (Gtr. 1). The album's solo guitar is also further processed, splitting the signal and routing it through an additional distortion device—possibly even routing the signal back into an input mixing board channel with the gain up full, as the distortion is not a smooth guitar-type distortion, but rather a completely broken-up and almost unrecognizable fuzz tone. This aspect has not been reproduced in the accompanying audio for the sake of clarity.

The solo utilizes the E minor pentatonic patterns throughout. It opens in box 4, with a characteristic Iommi 1 1/2 step bend from the root (E) up to the minor 3rd (G). In this case, it is a pre-bend type, meaning that you should push the string up to pitch *before* picking it, thereby eliminating any audible bend up. Thereafter, immediately release the bend back down to E and pull off to D, followed by a hammer back to E, resolving this minor pentatonic embellishment to the root. The remainder of the first four-measure solo phrase descends through the low extension of the E minor pentatonic box 4 shape (technically part of box 3).

The second four-measure phrase begins in the same region and rises into the upper reaches of box 4. Tony then blurs the natural phrase demarcation between measures 8 and 9 (measure 9 begins the next four-measure "parcel"), drawing upon his "continuous" style of phrasing by seamlessly shifting up into box 1, in twelfth position—a full two beats early. These notes act as "pick ups" into measure 9.

Notice the powerful melodic tension resulting from the 1/2 step bends (D up to D♯) interspersed between whole step bends (D up to E) in measure 9. The D♯s (major 7ths), achieved through string bending, lend a strong tonal contrast to the otherwise straight minor pentatonic stylings.

The solo attains its melodic peak in measure 10, with the high-register minor 3rd (G) to 4th (A) whole step bends on the first string. Thereafter, it meanders down incrementally through box 1 (with low extension) to the low octave root, and then back up to finally land upon the mid root (E) of the pattern.

Throughout the solo, all sixteenth notes are achieved with hammers, pulls, or slides, allowing the picking to stay fairly consistent in eighth notes.

19	Featured Guitars:
	Gtr. 1 meas. 1-16

20	Slow Demos:
	Gtr. 1 meas. 1-16

Fig. 9

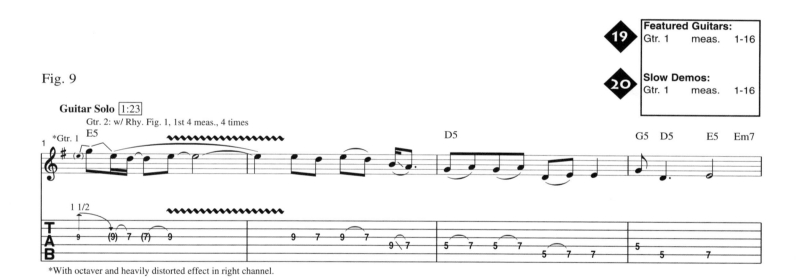

*With octaver and heavily distorted effect in right channel.

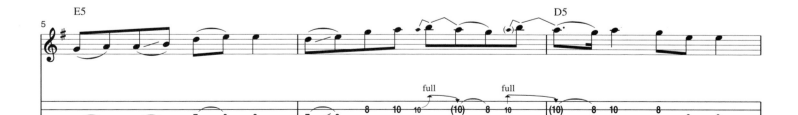

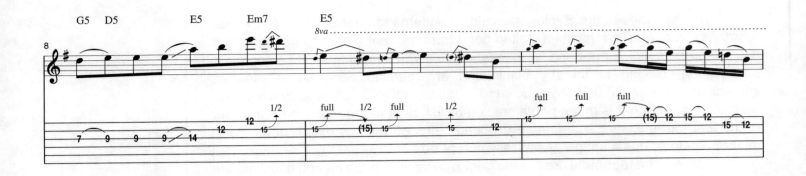

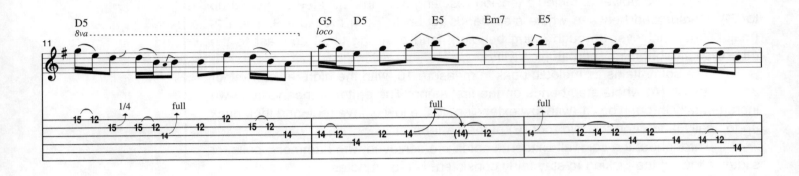

WAR PIGS (INTERPOLATING LUKE'S WALL)

Words and Music by Frank Iommi, John Osbourne, William Ward, and Terence Butler

Figure 10 — Preamble, Intro, Verse, and Interlude

"War Pigs," another grand-scale metal masterpiece, is the opening cut from *Paranoid*, and a standout Sabbath tune. Through powerful metaphors as well as direct statements, the band rails against and vilifies the military planners and politicians who conspire to send their innocent citizens into war and death. Compositionally, this song is on a par with—if not even more complex than—"Iron Man" and contains numerous signature elements.

The opening preamble offers a decidedly relaxed, triplet-based groove in 12/8 time. This time signature implies four "compound" beats per measure, and in that regard, is quite similar to 4/4 time. The difference lies in the fact that the natural subdivision of each beat is three (a triplet, or triple meter) while 4/4 subdivides beats into two (duple meter). Therefore, 12/8 is written with *three* eighth notes per beat, and since three eighth notes equal a dotted quarter note, the basic time value of a quarter note in 4/4 time (one full beat) actually appears written as a *dotted* quarter note in 12/8 time. Think very "laid back" as you play this part, then slow yourself down a bit more...a tempo of 37 beats per minute is slow indeed! In fact, it is good practice to tap out not only the compound beats (four per measure), but the full triplet subdivisions of each beat as well (twelve of these per measure), counting "*one*-two-three, *four*-five-six, *seven*-eight-nine, *ten*-eleven-twelve" or some reasonable equivalent.

Over this backing groove, the guitar lays down a shifting motif of E-D which builds gradually. The first E is played as a power chord (E5), while D is played as a vibratoed, single note. At the end of measure 2, pickups into the next two-measure phrase spell out an E major chord with the added major 3rd (G♯) tone. Note the use of the 4th (A) here as well, acting as a melodic suspension and temporarily implying Esus4. The tonality here—with E as tonal center and prominent D (minor 7th) notes as well as G♯ (major 3rd)—is that of E Mixolydian.

In measure 5, the 4th (A) functions as a passing tone up to the 5th (B) as the melodic tension rises. The next step up occurs in measures 6-8 where a compositional device called *diminution* is employed. Diminution is a technique whereby the time value of a motif is cut in half, so the phrases go by twice as fast and thereby provide yet another energy surge. (This is not the same as double time, as the tempo, or pulse, does not change speed.)

Finally, the leap is made to full speed ahead in measure 9, at the intro. Here, the meter abruptly changes to 4/4 at a new, faster tempo, and the opening D5-E5 motif from the preamble is stripped down to its barest form—space itself becoming the dominant, ear-catching aspect. This type of forward-leaning meter and tempo changes would eventually became a hallmark in progressive rock and metal.

Also of interest is the Sabbath structuring concept of an introduction section (in this case we have labeled it as "preamble") followed by a new section (in this case labeled "intro") which is found to utilize the same riff as in the following verse. This has the effect of establishing a "platform" first, to which vocals are then added on top.

As per usual, Sabbath follows the verse not with a chorus, but once again with an instrumental interlude. In this case, the interlude figure also incorporates the D5-E5 motif of the verse riff and simply augments it by filling in a portion of the space with a chromatically descending line of power chords: G5-F♯5-F5-E5. The effect is as if the interlude riff organically "grows" out of the verse riff. In particular, notice the strong leaning provided by the F5 (♭II) power chord held in the first half of measures 30, 32, and 33. Another groundbreaking tonal exercise, the ♭II chord (along with ♭V) would later come to dominate the heavier styles of metal in the 90s.

Fig. 10

sor - cer - er ___ of death's con - struc - tion. ___ In the fields the bod - ies

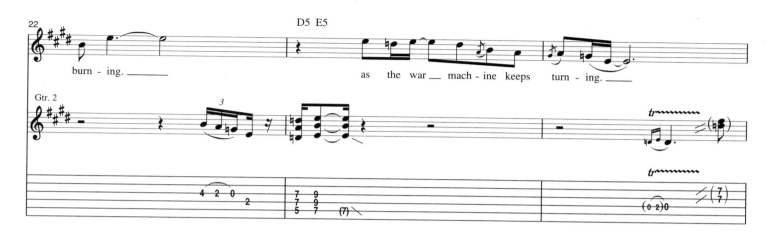

burn - ing. ___ as the war ___ mach - ine keeps turn - ing. ___

Gtr. 2

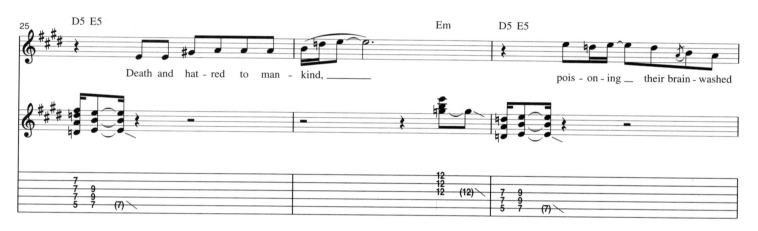

Death and hat - red to man - kind, ___ pois - on - ing ___ their brain - washed

Interlude

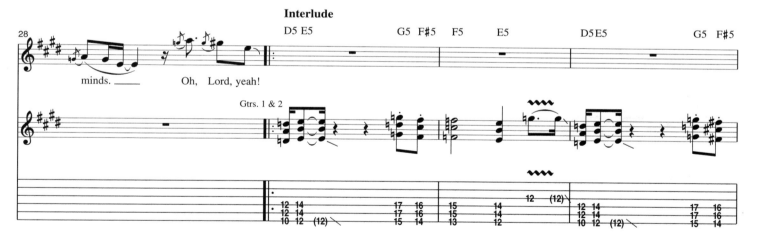

minds. ___ Oh, Lord, yeah!

Gtrs. 1 & 2

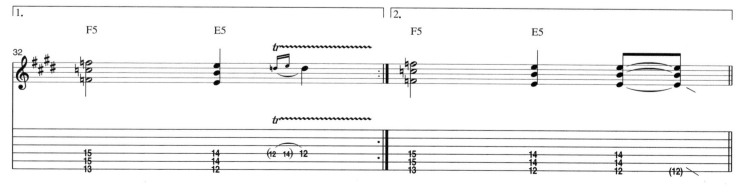

29

Figure 11 — Interlude and Bridge

Immediately after the final interlude of Figure 10, a second instrumental interlude emerges. This riff features churning, low E string palm-mutes juxtaposed against a G chord accent and slide at the twelfth fret (a signature Iommi-ism) on beat 2, and funky offbeat syncopations in beat 3. Play all the sixteenth-note low E palm mutes with downstrokes of the pick and attack the chord with an upstroke for maximum articulation. The final G note (E's minor 3rd) on beat 4 is played with a distinct finger vibrato (a fast series of small bends and releases that help to enliven a note). The riff overall draws upon the E minor pentatonic scale (E-G-A-B-D).

The bridge section (or secondary verse) enters in measure 5. Here the riff is altered but still retains its essential, chugging sixteenth-note nature and similar syncopation pattern. However, we find an E to D pull-off in place of the Em accent chord on beat 2, and this pull-off is restated on beat 4. The riff concludes with a bend at the second fret from the 2nd (F♯) to the minor 3rd (G), which smoothly releases back to F♯, producing a slightly "soured" version of the minor 3rd. (In the riff's previous incarnation, in the interlude measures 1-4, you'll remember that the final minor 3rd had been played with finger vibrato.) Tonally, the riff draws upon E minor pentatonic, with a hint of natural minor due to the presence of F♯ in the bend's release. However, as the vocal line repeatedly stresses G♯ (E's major 3rd), the overall tonality is that of E Mixolydian with the minor 3rd (G) sounding as an added "blue note," temporarily borrowed from the parallel minor.

After you learn these riffs, practice "falling into the groove" without unduly rushing the tempo—especially through the syncopated portion of the riffs. Repetitive groove playing like this requires a special type of "concentration endurance" which is gained only by practicing for long, unbroken repetitions.

	Featured Guitars:		
23	Gtr. 1	meas.	1-12
	Slow Demos:		
24	Gtr. 1	meas.	1; 5

Fig. 11

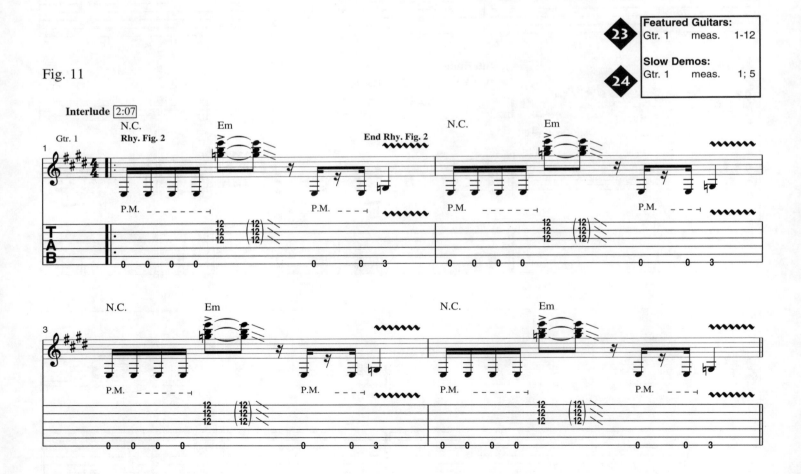

Figure 12 — Guitar Solo

This splendid guitar moment is one of Iommi's highlights. He opens with a composed thematic idea which draws upon the dominant notes of the bridge melody, using the E Mixolydian mode (E-F#-G#-A-B-C#-D) against a low E string *pedal tone*. Notice especially the sweet, bright quality of G# (major 3rd). Rhythmically, it is presented in a "three against four" approach. That is, he plays one note picked, slides to a second note, then hits the low E string for a third note. This three note sequence is then repeated consistently, over a rhythm of four notes per beat (sixteenths) creating a hemiola-style rhythmic interaction. This interesting rhythmic effect has been seized upon and reflects an important part of the metal lexicon.

In measure 4, Tony leaves Mixolydian behind and shifts gears into E minor pentatonic, beginning in the venerable "blues box" (box 1), in twelfth position. Play the sixteenth-note triplets in measures 4-5 with a downstroke raking approach, similar to that of a strum. Notice also the additional Gtr. 2 splitting off into improvised mayhem in measures 5-9.

Measure 7 offers the melodic peak point of the solo—a high A note played on the first string as a result of a whole step bend up from G at the fifteenth fret. He then cascades down to a breaking point, to "regroup," in measure 9. Notice the rhythmically consistent picking of sixteenth-notes running nearly throughout, with added pull-offs generating the thirty-second note bursts. Remember, each group of two thirty-second notes (with three beams) takes up the same amount of time as a single sixteenth note (with two beams).

Iommi again takes up the gauntlet in measure 10, this time in E minor pentatonic box 4, with a whole step bend up and out of the pentatonic confines to F# (the 2nd). Measure 11 restates the prominent motif established earlier in measures 4-5, drawing the solo together as a compositional device.

Then things get totally crazy in measures 12-13. Here the E (root) to F# (2nd) whole step bend motif is blended together with a D-E trill, and the entire sequence is repeated in the same three-against-four rhythmic pattern we saw first in the opening theme (measures 1-3). This rhythmic aspect may not be immediately apparent due to the complexity of the repeated pattern. However, if one regards the bend and release as one event (as it truly is when played at this speed)—and therefore combined the time of those two notes together into one—it would look like a single sixteenth note. Then, notice that the time value of the trill is an eighth note—the equivalent of two sixteenths. Put both of these together and the total time for one bend/trill combination is the equivalent of three sixteenths. When that is repeated over and over, exactly the same rhythmic interaction will occur. The bend will appear at different points relative to the underlying pulse: First on the downbeat of 1, then on the fourth sixteenth of beat 1, then the upbeat of beat 2, then the second sixteenth of beat 3. At that point (three full beats) the pattern has come full circle and the bend will become "reacquainted" with the downbeat starting on beat 4.

This lick is a killer, no doubt about it. Rumor has it that this section was actually done by slowing down the tape and recording it at a slower tempo (and in a correspondingly lower key), then playing it back at full speed. This author spent some time on it—more than any other single section of this recording—which may seem to support that hypothethis. Yet this also shows that while it is difficult, nevertheless, it *can* be done.

Tony closes out the solo in his inimitable fashion of backing out the same way he came in (restating his original thematic element). However, as is also typical of his improvisationally-based style, the restatements are not exact duplicates but are improvised variations on the original. This comes in measures 17-18 in the form of a 1/2 step bend from D# (major 7th) to E and a slight, "sour" release, applied to the original three-against-four rhythmic pattern.

Finally to wrap it up, the guitar joins the rhythm section in alternating E5-D5 power chords, recalling the building motif of the preamble.

	Featured Guitars:		
25	Gtr. 1	meas.	1-22

	Slow Demos:		
26	Gtr. 1	meas.	1-18

Fig. 12

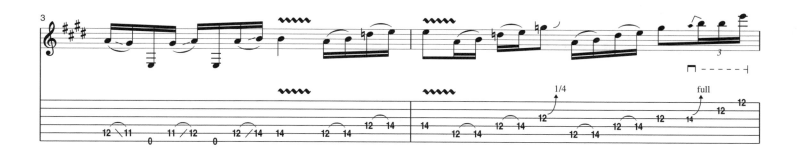

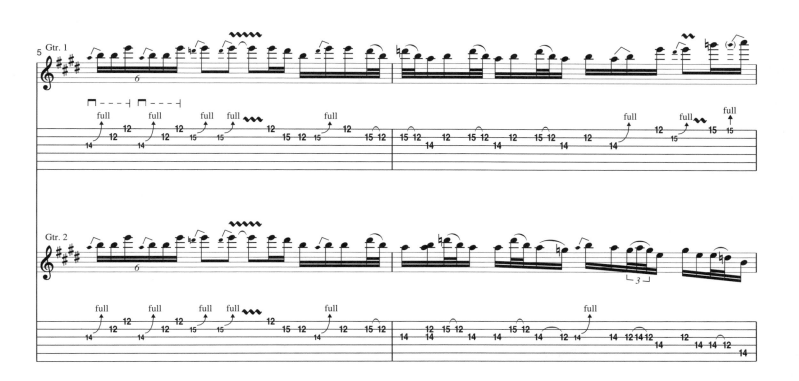

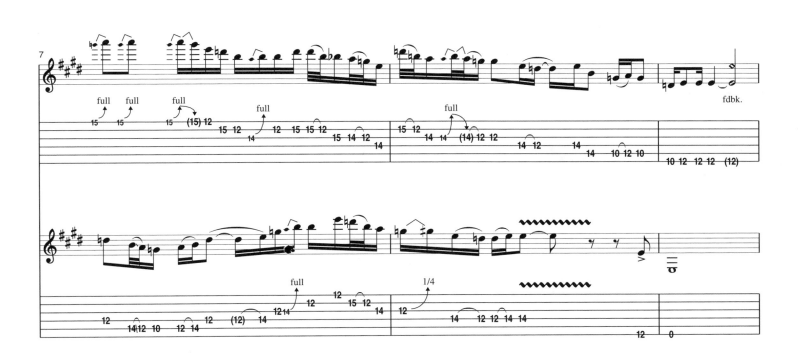

pitch: E

SWEET LEAF

Words and Music by Frank Iommi, John Osbourne, William Ward, and Terence Butler

Figure 13 — Intro, Verse, and Interlude

With their creativity in high gear, Black Sabbath continued to pick up momentum with the release of their third album, *Master of Reality*, in July, 1971. Selling over 500,000 units in the US before even being released, it quickly attained a spot at #8 on the US album charts—the best US showing of any Sabbath album— and achieved platinum status (sales over 1 million copies) shortly thereafter, also helping to propel the first two releases likewise.

On the heels of the drug-extolling counterculture of the 1960s, "Sweet Leaf," the album's opening cut, is a drug anthem promoting the mind-expanding virtues of marijuana. The arrangement seems targeted toward this end through the use of a highly repetitive one-measure riff acting as both intro and verse and producing a lulling, hypnotic, ostinato effect. The production also supports this mood with a smooth, laid back, almost distant quality to the mix.

The main riff is in the key of A minor. Two eighth-note A5 power chords cement the tonal center, followed by chromatic descending motion through D5-D♭5-C5. Quarter note C5-D5 chords wraps up the short one-measure motif. For maximum effect, try cranking your distortion level up all the way, and play with a softer picking technique along with a somewhat slower than normal strumming technique.

True to their unique style of song form, the interlude here once again functions as a chorus replacement. The chord sequence here (A5-G5-C5-E5-A5) utilizes a minor pentatonic style progression—the root movement can be seen to draw upon four (A-C-E-G) of the five tones of A minor pentatonic (A-C-D-E-G). The slide down from the highest chord, E5, should be pronounced.

Fig. 13

Featured Guitars:
Gtr. 1   meas.   1-22

Slow Demos:
Gtr. 1   meas.   3-4

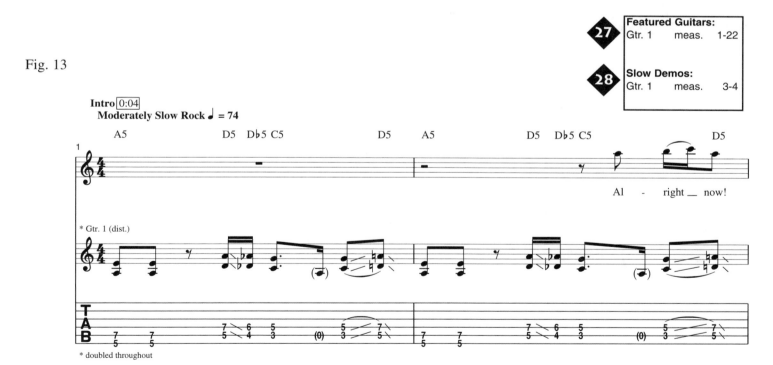

Interlude

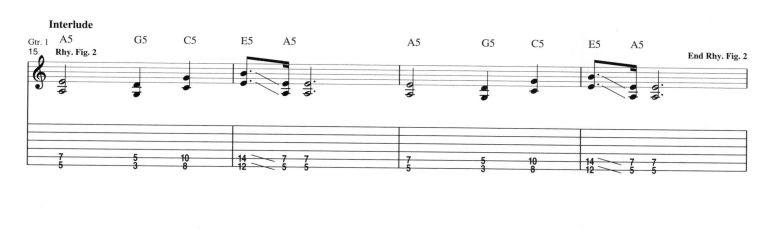

CHILDREN OF THE GRAVE

Words and Music by Frank Iommi, William Ward, John Osbourne, and Terence Butler

Figure 14 — Intro, Verse, and Interlude

"Children of the Grave" is a significant landmark as it signaled the beginning of Sabbath's pioneering experimentation with ultra-low C# tuning. This tuning would come to dominate much of the band's sound over the next several years and would help to set apart their music even further from mainstream standards. In recent years, many modern metal bands have reached back to Sabbath's lead, and begun to incorporate a variety of similar ultra-low tunings.

Use the tuning notes given on track 29 of the audio to tune your strings down to C# tuning. Because every string is lowered, they all still retain the same relative tuning to each other—they simply sound 1 1/2 steps lower. To keep things simple, we still refer to all the notes and chords as if we were in standard tuning. So, for example, we call the open sixth string an "E" even though technically it sounds at the pitch of C#. Ideally, heavier string gauges are recommended for using a low slack tuning such as this, since this enables the strings to hold their pitch more reliably and "flap" somewhat less. In any case, you'll find that string bending offers significantly less resistance, and you'll have to be careful not to overbend strings.

"Children of the Grave" uses a triplet-based groove. Notice the shuffle symbol in parentheses after the tempo indication at the start of the song. This means that whenever you see eighth notes, they are to be played as a shuffle, or swing. That is, the second eighth note is played on the last *third* of the beat, rather than on the upbeat, or midpoint between beats (as would be the case without the shuffle symbol). The essential rhythmic motif at the core of the song is a five-note figure played on the open sixth string. Pick down...down-up-down-up so this figure can be repeated identically over and over.

The band enters with the main riff in measures 2-3. This consists of three repetitions of the rhythmic motif on E, with added octave embellishments, followed by quarter-note chord punches on C5-B5 (bVI-V). As the driving rhythm motif continues underneath as an open sixth string pedal, Gtr. 2 steps to the forefront and outlines an E5-G5-C5-D5 (i-bIII-bVI-bVII) chord progression. This powerful E natural minor (Aeolian mode) progression functions essentially as the song's "instrumental chorus" later, after each verse.

Rhythm Figure 3 (measures 14-15) enters for the verse, and consists of an altered version of the original main riff. The rhythmic motif and octave embellishments remain intact, but the previous C5-B5 chord punches are omitted in favor of a catchy, offbeat chord accent on G5 (bIII). At the same time, Gtr. 3 adds background ambience in the form of a vibratoed, unison string bend, on a high G note.

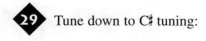

29 Tune down to C# tuning:

Tune Down 1 1/2 Steps:

①= C#   ④= B

②= G#   ⑤= F#

③= E   ⑥= C#

Fig. 14

1. Rev - o - lu - tion in _____ their minds, _____ the

Fill 1
Gtr. 3 (dist.)
8va **End Fill 1**

full
15
18

Gtrs. 1 & 2 **Rhy. Fig. 3** **End Rhy. Fig. 3**
P.M.

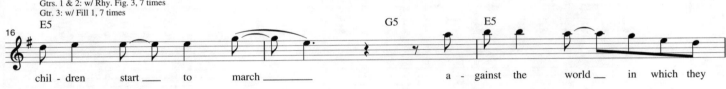

Gtrs. 1 & 2: w/ Rhy. Fig. 3, 7 times
Gtr. 3: w/ Fill 1, 7 times

chil - dren start _____ to march _____ a - gainst the world _____ in which they

have to live _____ in. Oh, the hate that's in _____ their hearts. _____ They're

tired of be - ing pushed _____ a - round _____ and told _____ just what _____ to do. _____

_____ They'll fight the world _____ un - til _____ they've won _____ and

40

love   comes   flow - ing   through. _____   Yeah! _____

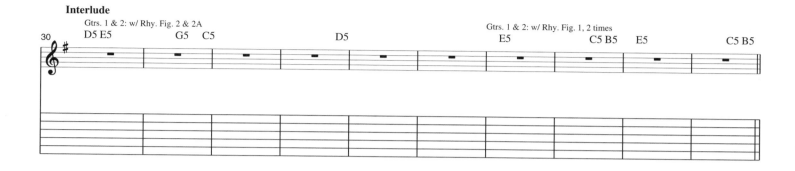

Figure 15 — Interlude and Bridge

An unusual instrumental section functions as the song's bridge. But not before a fast, climbing blues riff enters, which the entire band plays together in unison. Here, the drums accompany the guitar and bass, playing "stop time" in the rests, instead of keeping a beat throughout.

The first riff rises up the E blues scale (E-G-A-B♭-B-D) in measure 1. Then measure 2 utilizes the notes of the same scale in a slightly altered sequence, ending on the 4th (A) rather than on the octave root (E). This sets up a question/answer-style phrase, or *ABAB* form.

The bridge section begins in measure 3, with a half-time drum feel. This means that the perceived pulse is half the speed that it was previously. However, in this case, the music is still written in reference to the original tempo. In other words, a whole note will be the length of four beats at the original tempo, but only two "half time" beats. (The half time beats will fall on the "old" beats 1 and 3.)

The tonality of the bridge section is quite interesting and inventive. Here Sabbath flirts with a *diminished tonality*—another heavy rock first, which later death metal bands would come to incorporate "religiously." The opening E5 power chord anchors the tonal center. Then we see G5, built upon the minor 3rd (G) and suggesting an E minor tonality. Measure 5 adds B♭5, drawing upon the tritone interval relative to the key center, E. Together, the prominent use of the root (E), minor 3rd (G), and diminished 5th (B♭), can be seen to imply an E diminished tonality.

This is further reinforced in measure 6, where Iommi slides up from B♭5 to B5, then again from C♯5 to D5, in transit back to E5. As the E (half-whole) diminished scale (E-F-G-A♭-B♭-B-C♯-D) actually consists of alternating half- and whole-step intervals, the root movement here follows that scale exactly. Notice the "twisted," non-diatonic sound here. The diminished scale has eight tones per octave (octatonic) rather than the typical seven tones of the diatonic (major or minor) scales.

In the second variation of the bridge riff (measures 7-10), we see a C♯5 substituted in place of B♭5. As C♯ (or D♭) is actually the double-flatted 7th tone of an E diminished 7th chord, this functions nicely as an alternative pattern which still maintains the same diminished feel.

Fig. 15

Tune Down 1 1/2 Steps:
① = C# ④ = B
② = G# ⑤ = F#
③ = E ⑥ = C#

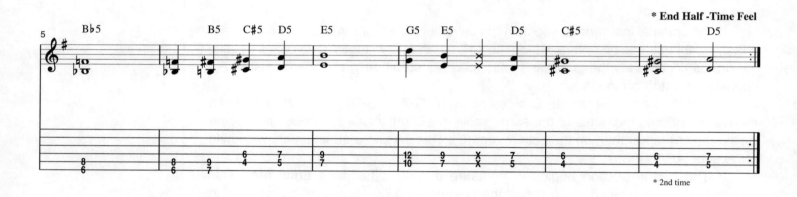

* 2nd time

INTO THE VOID

Words and Music by Frank Iommi, William Ward, John Osbourne, and Terence Butler

Figure 16 — Preamble

"Into the Void" is a science fiction-style account of a future where pollution, war, hate, and fear have ravaged the planet and global environmental catastrophe looms. In an effort to save mankind, a small group of explorers are sent to begin life anew on an unspoiled planetary home.

The opening introduction section, or preamble, which connects to the body of "Into the Void" was originally given the separate and charming title "Death Mask" on the album. But all subsequent CD releases have combined the two into a single track labeled "Into the Void." Figure 16 shows the main portions of this opening section.

Once again in the ultra-low C# tuning, the riff utilizes the E blues scale (E-G-A-B♭-B-D). Notice the out-of-key passing tone, D#, as the top voicing descends chromatically from the octave root (E), to D# (major 7th), to D natural (minor 7th).

Measure 3 features a hammer-pull sequence with an interesting rhythmic twist. As the 1 1/2 beat motif is repeated, it falls against the beat differently—first beginning on the downbeat of 1, then beginning on the upbeat of 2, and on the third time beginning on the downbeat of 4. The three repetitions are bracketed in Figure 16 to help you see the rhythmic interaction.

Measure 5 starts the next musical section of the preamble. Borrowing temporarily from the parallel major key, we see E major chords with the inclusion of G# (major 3rd). This relatively rare concession to major key tonality only slightly brightens the sound; due to the ultra-low tuning, it remains quite deep and heavy. The next D chords are given extra low end thickness by virtue of their 5th tone (A) appearing at the bottom of the chord (second inversion). Also, notice the D# passing tone again appearing in measure 6, this time in a new riff context.

Measures 11-12 close out the secondary portion of the preamble with a C5-B5 (♭VI-V) cadence, which sets up a V-I pull back to the tonic, E, for another time through the opening riff.

Fig. 16

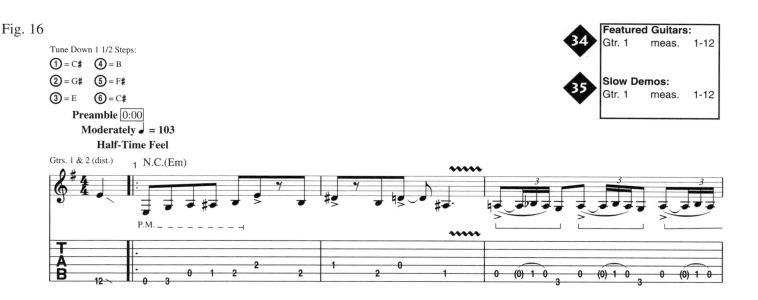

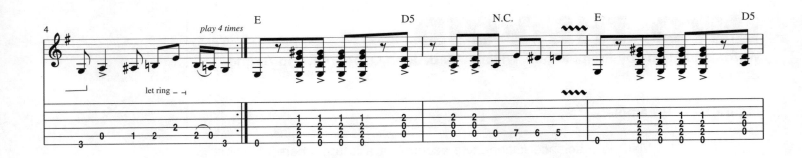

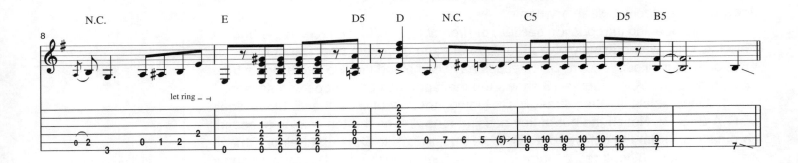

Figure 17 — Intro and Verse

At 1:14, the tempo shifts abruptly as the guitars introduce Riff A—the main riff of "Into the Void." A hammer-on transforms the initial D-over-E dyads into octave Es, while a palm-muted pedal tone chunks along on the sixth string. Play with all downstrokes of the pick.

Be careful not to overbend the 1/2-step bend at the end of measure 2. With a low, slack tuning such as this, the 1/2-step bend requires only a very slight amount of pressure to pull it to the correct pitch. Also, notice that the vibrato is to be applied to the bent note—After bending at the fifth fret up to pitch (B♭), release the bend slightly, then push it back up two or three times in rapid succession before finally releasing to A.

The riff functions as the underpinning of the verse as well, but with a slight alteration. Notice the added bend and release from D at the fifth fret in measure 3.

Fig. 17

Tune Down 1 1/2 Steps:
① = C♯   ④ = B
② = G♯   ⑤ = F♯
③ = E   ⑥ = C♯

	Featured Guitars:	
36	Gtr. 1	meas. 1-17
	Slow Demos:	
37	Gtr. 1	meas. 1-2

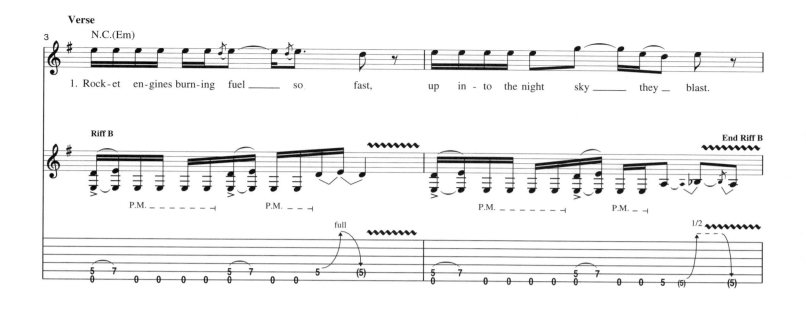

Verse

1. Rock-et en-gines burn-ing fuel _____ so fast, up in-to the night sky _____ they _ blast.

Gtrs. 1 & 2: w/ Riff B, 3 times, simile

Through the un - i - verse the en - gines whine. Could it be the end of man _____ and _ time?

Back on earth the flame of life _____ burns low. Ev - 'ry-where is mis - er - y _____ and _ woe. Pol -

lu - tion kills the air, the land, _____ and sea. Man pre-pares to meet his des - ti - ny, yeah. _

Gtrs. 1 & 2:
w/ Riff A

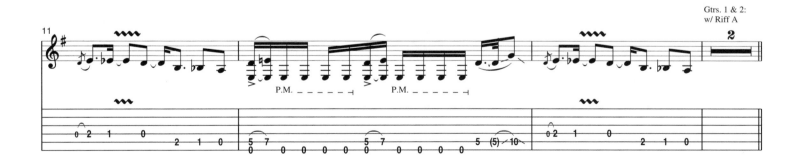

Figure 18 — Guitar Solo, Interlude, Outro-Solo, Outro

The guitar solo displays Iommi's trademark technique of tracking two solos which begin in unison (measures 1-3) and later break apart in improvisational excess (measures 4-6).

Measure 1 starts in the low extension of box 4 (also known as the secondary position) of E minor pentatonic in the fifth position. It quickly shifts up into box 4 "proper," leading into measure 2. What appears to be a 1 1/2 step bend up from the root (E) in measure two falls slightly short of the target pitch and results in a 1 1/4 step bend, giving it an odd blues-inspired tension falling between the "cracks" of the notes. In measures 4-5, the bend recurs in its expected 1 1/2 step (minor 3rd) interval.

At the interlude, beginning in measure 7, the guitars regroup and play a powerful secondary riff along with the bass guitar for four measures. After this, a series of stop-time accents set off the next eight measures with guitar fills building throughout. The first four fills (measures 11-14) feature slides with vibratoed bends rising incrementally. The peak notes are—in order—B♭ (diminished 5th), D♭ (♭♭7th), E♭ (major 7th), and F (minor 2nd).

The next four fills (measures 15-18) put forth a series of minor pentatonic barrages, with Gtrs. 1 & 2 trading off in a Jimmy Page-inspired moment. The first three fills are all played in the E minor pentatonic "blues box," or box 1, at the twelfth fret. The final 1 1/2 step overbend occurs on the third string in box 4.

After that brief compositional interruption, the guitar solo(s) resume in improvised fashion. Again shifting fluently between boxes 4 and 1, Iommi builds in his usual fashion—beginning in the lower register of box 4 (measures 19-20), shifting up into box 1 (measure 21), peaking with a high G (minor 3rd) to A (4th) whole step bend (measure 22) at the top of box 1, then riding out the remaining measures with blues licks (measures 23-24).

The Outro is a restatement of the previous interlude riff, which repeats four times, ending on a decisive final E note with added reverb.

Fig. 18

Tune Down 1 1/2 Steps:
① = C♯   ④ = B
② = G♯   ⑤ = F♯
③ = E   ⑥ = C♯

Guitar Solo 4:46

38
Featured Guitars:		
Gtr. 1	meas.	1-14
Gtr. 2	meas.	15
Gtr. 1	meas.	16
Gtr. 2	meas.	17
Gtr. 1	meas.	18-28

39
Slow Demos:		
Gtr. 1	meas.	1-7
Gtr. 2	meas.	15
Gtr. 1	meas.	16
Gtr. 2	meas.	17
Gtr. 1	meas.	19-24

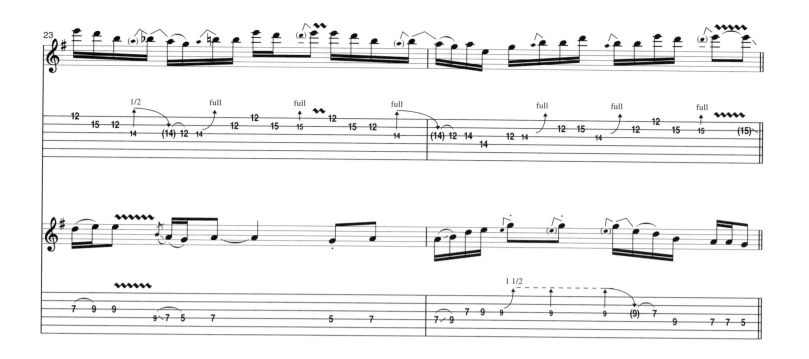

Outro
N.C.
Gtrs. 1 & 2

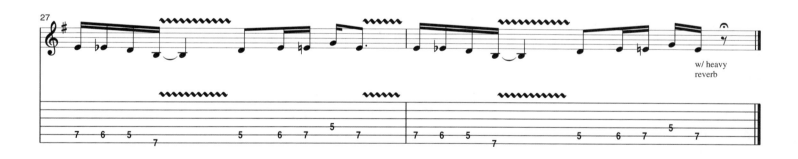

SUPERNAUT

Words and Music by Frank Iommi, Terence Butler, William Ward, and John Osbourne

Figure 19 — Intro, Verse, and Interlude

With the release of *Black Sabbath Vol. 4*, the band had put out an impressive four albums in three short years, on top of a relentless touring schedule in both the United States and Europe. This feat alone deserves significant recognition, yet in addition to this, the four members continued throughout this period to create groundbreaking new material and progress markedly—not simply rehashing the same ideas. "Supernaut" is a prime example and prominent track from *Black Sabbath Vol. 4*.

The lyrics paint imagistic portraits of drug-induced astral travels (much along the same lines as in Ozzy's later solo effort, "Flying High Again"). In support of this other-worldly atmosphere, the guitar sets the stage with a single-note line which at once sounds familiar yet retains a certain unusual, distinctive quality. The riff's odd nature is imparted due to the creative use of slides and open strings in Sabbath's favorite new ultra-low tuning.

The tonal center of the riff is established with the opening E note played on the fifth string, seventh fret. The following D at the fifth fret is the minor 7th tone, while the open A string functions as the 4th. When the riff rises to the fourth string, following the same physical pattern, the seventh fret (A) is the 4th, the fifth fret (G) is the minor 3rd and the open fourth string (D) functions as the minor 7th. Taken together, these notes spell out E minor pentatonic (E-G-A-B-D) minus the 5th tone, B. Play all the fretted notes with the same finger (this author used the second finger) to help give the grace-note slides their proper feel.

In measures 7-10, Gtr. 2 adds a parallel harmony line—a new venture for Sabbath. Over Gtr. 1's E and D, we see G♯ and F♯, both major 3rd intervals. As G♯ borrows temporarily from the parallel major key of E major, we hear the distinct "twisting" quality of a mixed major/minor tonality. The harmony is further skewed by the following D♯ tone played against the open A string, producing the turbulent and hair-raising tritone (augmented 4th) as a harmonic interval. A similar harmony approach functions over the remainder of the riff, simply shifted up a string.

Next, the verse riff kicks in, utilizing a second inversion power chord E5/B. With the 5th tone (B) at the bottom of the chord, and played in ultra-low tuning, this colors the normally consonant E5 chord with a dark, low-end dissonance. More creatively employed slides follow, performed with palm mutes. These function not as pitches at all, but rather, utilize the slide quality itself as an integral part of the riff. The peak note is D, but you should regard this note as a rough "target point" for how high up the neck the slide should go—you should not hear D as a pitch. Also, when starting of the slide, be sure that your finger is moving as it hits the string while you pick. Otherwise you will first hear an unwanted lower note followed by the slide. Here, you want to achieve a rising slide for the entire duration of the eighth note. There should be no discernable pitch.

Fig. 19

Tune Down 1 1/2 Steps:
①= C♯   ④= B
②= G♯   ⑤= F♯
③= E   ⑥= C♯

	Featured Guitars:		
40	Gtr. 1	meas.	3-34
41	**Slow Demos:**		
	Gtr. 1	meas.	3-6;
			11-12

SABBATH, BLOODY SABBATH

Words and Music by Frank Iommi, John Osbourne, William Ward, and Terence Butler

Figure 20 — Intro, Verse, and Interlude

The recording of *Sabbath Bloody Sabbath*, the band's fifth effort, was the occasion of a famous band story. They had set up in an old English castle to compose and record a bit. Strange things began to happen right away. A fire spread unexpectedly from the fireplace, and Ozzy, sleeping nearby, woke at the last moment and narrowly escaped. Shortly thereafter, several members of the band witnessed an unknown man walk into a room, and upon following him, found that the room was empty and the only other door out of it was locked from the inside. They began to tell each other horrifying stories, and in the end, were all so scared they had to leave the castle that same night!

The album was finally completed (in the welcome security of the recording studio) and released in December, 1973. The title track shows a broadening influence in terms of arrangement and textures. Acoustic guitars were implemented in a significant way, and Rick Wakeman (Yes) was brought on board for keyboard duties.

Again played in the slack tuning of C♯ (down 1 1/2 steps), the riff makes clever use of the open fifth and fourth strings as a D5 dyad, hammering straight onto the E5 in seventh position. This offers a subtle but noticeable variation on the basic D5-E5 motion that Sabbath uses so much. Also, palm mutes are maintained entirely on the fifth and fourth strings—forgoing the more common low E pedal tone standard. Overall, the riff follows an E5-C5-D5-E5-G5-E5 (i-♭VI-♭VII-i-♭III-i) progression, spelling out the E natural minor scale (Aeolian mode).

Structurally, this tune is somewhat of a departure from Sabbath's norm, as it includes a vocal-driven, chorus-type section which acts as a lower-energy point, counterbalancing the main riff with acoustic textures. Clean electric guitars (Gtrs. 2 & 3) add relaxed pentatonic-style melodies over the six-string acoustic guitar (Gtr. 4) which strums a cycling Am9-G/D progression. In measure 33, the G/D chord appears as a Gmaj7/D, lending a jazz-inspired feel. Measures 39-40 replace the G/D chord with a revolving D-A progression over a D string pedal tone which functions to build back into the original E minor riff.

Featured Guitars:

Gtr. 1	meas.	1-24
Gtr. 4	meas.	25-40
Gtr. 5	meas.	41-48

Slow Demos:

Gtr. 1	meas.	1-4;
Gtr. 4	meas.	25-40;
Gtr. 5	meas.	41-44

Fig. 20

Verse

Gtr. 1: w/ Rhy. Fig. 1, 4 times

D5 E5 — D5 E5 — N.C. — C5 — D5 — E5 — G5 — E5

You see right through dis - tort - ed eyes, ___ you know you have to ___ learn. ___

D5 E5 — D5 E5 — N.C. — C5 — D5 — E5 — G5 — E5

The ex - e - cu - tion of your mind, ___ you real - ly have to ___ turn. ___

D5 E5 — D5 E5 — N.C. — C5 — D5 — E5 — G5 — E5

The race is run, the book is read, the end be - gins to ___ show. ___

D5 E5 — D5 E5 — N.C. — C5 — D5 — E5 — G5 — E5

The truth is out, the lies are old, but you know what to ___ know. ___

Chorus

Gtr. 1 tacet

Am9 — G/D — Gtr. 3: w/ Fill 1

No - bod - y ___ will e - ver let you ___ know

Gtr. 2 (elec.)
p
w/ clean tone
mf

Gtr. 4 (acous.)
mf

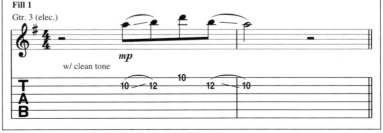

Fill 1
Gtr. 3 (elec.)
mp
w/ clean tone

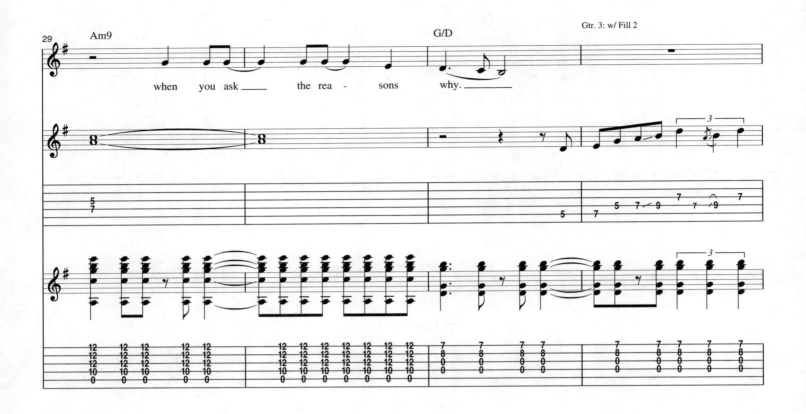

when you ask ___ the rea - sons why. ___

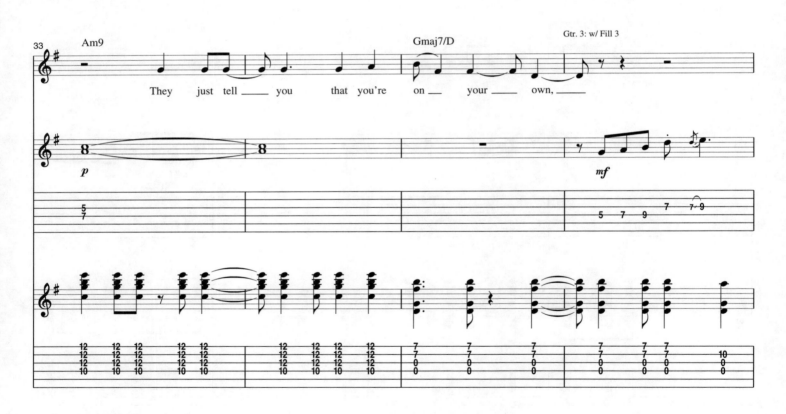

They just tell ___ you that you're on ___ your ___ own, ___

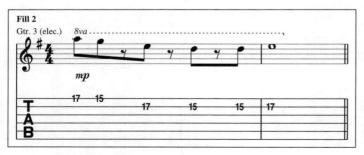

Interlude

SYMPTOM OF THE UNIVERSE
Words and Music by Frank Iommi, John Osbourne, William Ward, and Terence Butler

Figure 21 — Intro, Verse, and Interlude

"Symptom of the Universe" is a powerhouse track from the band's sixth album, *Sabotage*. Released in July, 1975, this marked the end of the first stage of Black Sabbath. Later, in the following year, many of the top songs from this era of the band's development would find additional success through the release of the compilation double-album, *We Sold Our Soul for Rock N Roll*. As the songlist had to be trimmed considerably to accommodate the limited time available on two LPs, "Symptoms" was not included. Nevertheless, this song was a live-show highlight and offers a glimpse of several important signature elements of the band's unique style.

Tony actually played "Symptom of the Universe" in two different ways. On the album (studio version) he uses the low C♯ tuning and plays it in the key of G, at the third fret. However, for live shows (on video) he can be seen playing the song in standard tuning, using the key of E (open position.) Either method will result in the same absolute pitch of E. Here, we will focus on the studio album version, using low C♯ tuning and playing in the key of G.

The riff (measures 1-4) opens the tune with relentless, driving intensity. A palm-muted G at the third fret hammers out a fast-paced eighth-note groove. The D♭5 chord, filling measure 2, is displaced forward a half-beat, or single eighth note. This G to D♭ root movement creates the same twisted tritone interval that we saw early on, in the band's namesake tune. A slight variation of the motif appears the second time around (measure 3). An octave G5 chord, played on strings 3 and 4, presages the D♭5 by one full beat. This riff also functions at the heart of the verse, with the vocal melody further enhancing the already strange tonal movement with odd chromatic motion.

An interlude section follows the verse, utilizing the chords F5-D♭5-C5. This is slightly different from the normal Sabbath interlude, inasmuch as it does contain a vocal part. But as this consists of a single, non-lyrically significant word ("Yeah") we can safely consider it an interlude. (The alternative would be to regard it as a chorus.) The F5 power chord is played as a three-string power chord rooted on string 4—a rare chord shape in Iommi's repertoire.

The overall tonality (incorporating G, D♭5, F5, and C5) seems to elude quick categorization as to the key. It does not fit neatly into G minor, which might be a good initial guess after having witnessed Sabbath's penchant for the Aeolian minor mode. Here, we see perhaps the first use of the *Locrian mode* in heavy metal. (In this case, G Locrian.) Originally regarded as too odd to be useful by the Greeks, the Locrian mode was actually included by the highly-organized Romans in an effort to account for all the seven theoretically possible modes, even if it had no practical use. This was the case for many centuries—until quite recent times. Black Sabbath helped resurrect the ignored mode and put it to use in heavy rock, where it would eventually become part of the musical vocabulary of the very meanest forms of metal—the thrash and death metal of the 1980s and 1990s.

Fig. 21

Tune Down 1 1/2 Steps:
① = C♯   ④ = B
② = G♯   ⑤ = F♯
③ = E   ⑥ = C♯

Featured Guitars:
Gtr. 1   meas.   1-40

Slow Demos:
Gtr. 1   meas.   1-4

HEAVEN AND HELL

Words by Ronnie James Dio, Music by Ronnie James Dio, Terence Butler, Anthony Iommi, and William Ward

Figure 22 — Intro, Verse, and Chorus

In 1977, Ozzy left the band due to a culmination of personal problems including alcohol and drug abuse as well as the death of his father and divorce from his first wife. In response, Sabbath brought ex-Fleetwood Mac member Dave Walker on board as vocalist and began working on the *Never Say Die* album. This lineup was short-lived, however, as Ozzy would return to finish the recording (released October, 1978) and sing on the subsequent tour. All was still not well, though; Ozzy and company finally parted ways again in early 1979.

As a replacement, Sabbath enlisted American singer and ex-Rainbow member Ronnie James Dio. This collaboration would breath new life into the band and result in the two prominent albums *Heaven and Hell*, in 1980, and later, *Mob Rules*, in 1981. Another personnel change also occurred at this time. Before Dio joined the band, Geezer Butler had left the band briefly and Geoff Nichols was brought on board to play bass. But when Geezer returned, Geoff moved over to keyboards—a duty he has retained since that time.

"Heaven and Hell," the 1980 album's title track, evidences some significant departures from the older-style Sabbath, as Dio was a driving force and dominant ego is his own right. In 1980, Dio is quoted, saying, "Why shouldn't I tamper around with Sabbath songs? I'm the singer now, and forgive me for saying so, but I'll do things my own damn way." Indeed! We see a stronger chorus form emerge in "Heaven and Hell," and the band experiments with a wider variety of dynamics. Several other significant changes include the tuning, which is now $E^\flat$ (still an "across the board" slack tuning, but down only 1/2 step rather than down 1 1/2 steps). Also, producer Martin Birch achieves a bigger, fuller, and more modern 1980s mix with punchier drum tones and thicker guitars. The formula wasn't completely revamped, however, as Tony Iommi's driving riffs still clearly cement the song in the familiar Sabbath tradition, not to mention the fact that "Heaven and Hell" is in the same epic vein as previous Sabbath works like "Iron Man."

The opening riff of "Heaven and Hell" recalls the minor mode approach played in E as used in "Sabbath Bloody Sabbath," "Children of the Grave," and "Snowblind"—although the $E^\flat$ tuning causes it to sound at a higher absolute pitch here, and therefore produces a different overall quality. The root movement of the power chord sequence walks up E natural minor from the root (E) to the 2nd (F#), to the minor 3rd (G), then falls to the minor 6th (C) and closes on the minor 7th (D) which pulls back to the tonic (E) to start all over again. The two-measure motif is then repeated with a different ending, rising up to and back down from a high A5 power chord at the twelfth fret and closing on the tonic (E5). All chords are played as power chords, but with some notable variations. The opening and closing E5s are played at the seventh fret, fifth string, along with an added low E string. Also, the D5s are played open, providing a somewhat brighter character for the upbeat accent point in measure 2.

The guitars drop out entirely for the first verse, drawing down the dynamic level significantly and allowing the bass and vocals to carry the day. This in itself was a milestone arrangement idea for heavy metal in 1980. It also allows for a more powerful chorus entrance, as guitars blast in from nowhere on the C5-D5 cadence, which builds back to the tonic chord, E5. But the chorus still isn't a chorus in the usual sense—the lyric "It's heaven and hell" only arrives in passing, as a transitional feature between the C5-D5 portion into a new, secondary riff in E minor (measures 23-26), presented as an instrumental buffer between the chorus and the next verse.

This riff features a powerful marching-type rhythm which synchronizes perfectly with the bass, which is playing the same eighth-sixteenth-sixteenth "gallop" motif found within the verse. Notice how Gtrs. 1 & 2 split slightly in measure 23. Also witness the exclusive use of E natural minor (E-F#-G-A-B-C-D), and notice the G chord accents at the twelfth fret on beat 4 (Gtr. 1). This favorite Iommi trademark appeared also in "War Pigs," "Paranoid," and "N.I.B."

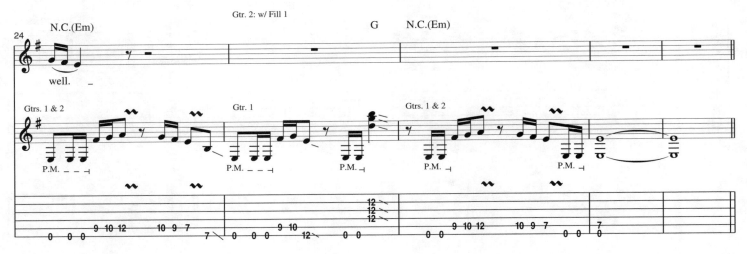

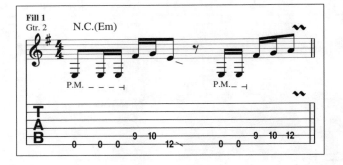

Figure 23 — Guitar Solo

An abbreviated form of the chorus gives way to the song's featured guitar solo—exceptionally well-composed and undoubtedly a highlight of Iommi's lead guitar-playing career. This solo consists of three distinct sections. Tony is clearly in no rush here and stretches it out, milking every bit of nuance in this masterful, full-minute-long lead guitar drama.

He begins with a series of long, carefully-paced phrases, offering plenty of space (measures 1-10). The long, slowly falling notes are further enhanced by a significant amount of reverb and a delay effect set at approximately 680 milliseconds, which produces echo repeats in roughly the equivalent time of quarter notes at this tempo. Bend quickly up to pitch and release only very gradually in measures 1-2. A well-placed low E note with echo repeats helps fill the following two measures of space where we are reoriented once again to the ever-present bass/drum groove. Pickups on beat 4 of measure 4 pull us into the next phrase (measures 5-8) where we find the signature Iommi tactic of employing the G chord played with one finger at the twelfth fret, over an E minor tonality. The remainder of this second phrase features E minor pentatonic box 4 blues licks with tasty vibrato applied on the 4ths (As). Measures 9-10 harken back to the first slow release motif seen at the opening of the solo, and function to neatly tie up this first section and set the stage for more action to follow.

In measure 11, he ratchets up the energy a notch for the second section of the solo. Building motivically, he applies a repeated sixteenth-sixteenth-eighth figure (filling in the gaps of the bass's eighth-sixteenth-sixteenth pattern) as he very deliberately steps down the scale in E minor pentatonic box 1, and into the low extension in measure 12. Tony then turns it diatonic in the second half of measure 12 with the inclusion of the 2nd (F#). After rising back up into the higher register once again, the rhythmic motive finally gives way to constant sixteenths, pushing the energy level incrementally one step higher.

Measure 17 is a two-beat measure which functions to pivot into the bridge chord progression (Am7-D-Dm7/A-C/G-Em). Over this, Gtr. 1 continues, entering the third and final section—the peak, or climax—of the guitar solo. Tony shifts gears to play fully diatonically here, drawing out a wistful, melodic sound (measures 18-21). Note the staggered, beautifully-executed rhythmic tension of the triplet figures. Measure 20 exhibits the melodic peak point of the solo, on the high B-note bend. Also, notice the blues-style phrasing in the end of this measure where, having established triplets as the routine, he then contradicts this by pulling four notes out of beat 4. The solo closes by once again drawing upon the opening motive—a bend followed by a long, slow release.

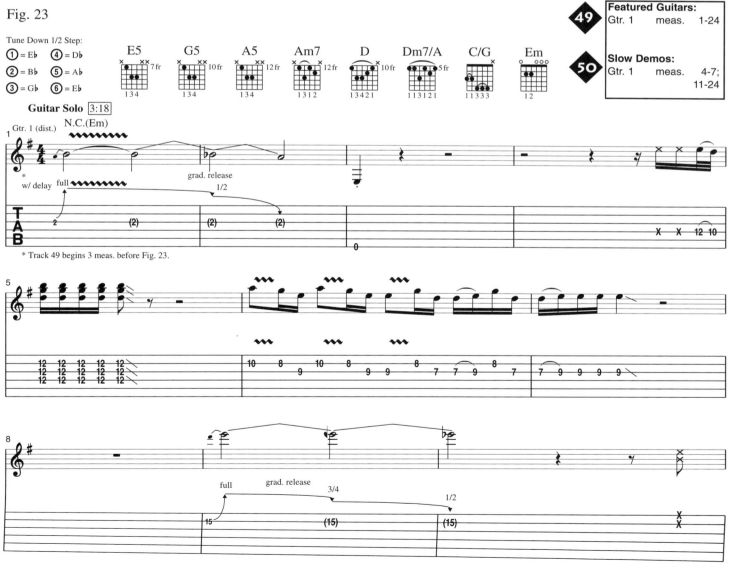

Fig. 23

* Track 49 begins 3 meas. before Fig. 23.

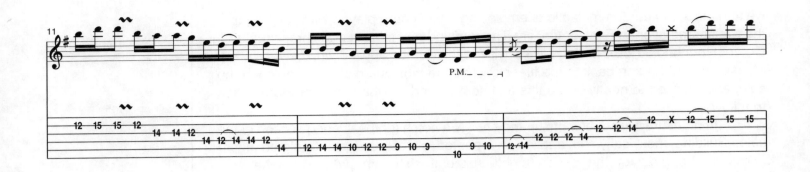

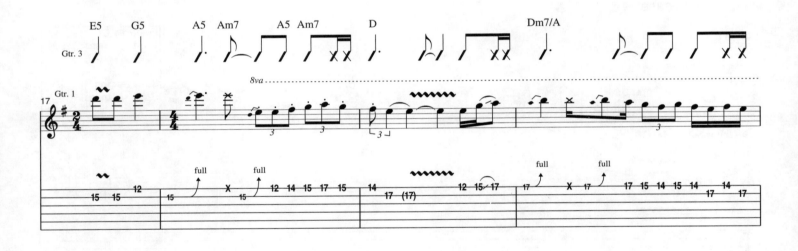

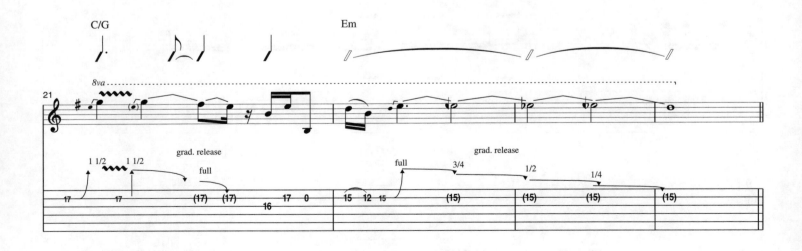

GUITAR NOTATION LEGEND

Guitar Music can be notated three different ways: on a *musical staff*, in *tablature*, and in *rhythm slashes*.

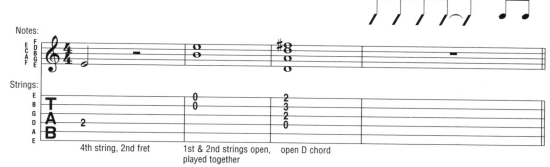

RHYTHM SLASHES are written above the staff. Strum chords in the rhythm indicated. Use the chord diagrams found at the top of the first page of the transcription for the appropriate chord voicings. Round noteheads indicate single notes.

THE MUSICAL STAFF shows pitches and rhythms and is divided by bar lines into measures. Pitches are named after the first seven letters of the alphabet.

TABLATURE graphically represents the guitar fingerboard. Each horizontal line represents a string, and each number represents a fret.

4th string, 2nd fret   1st & 2nd strings open, played together   open D chord

---

HALF-STEP BEND: Strike the note and bend up 1/2 step.

WHOLE-STEP BEND: Strike the note and bend up one step.

GRACE NOTE BEND: Strike the note and bend up as indicated. The first note does not take up any time.

SLIGHT (MICROTONE) BEND: Strike the note and bend up 1/4 step.

BEND AND RELEASE: Strike the note and bend up as indicated, then release back to the original note. Only the first note is struck.

PRE-BEND: Bend the note as indicated, then strike it.

VIBRATO: The string is vibrated by rapidly bending and releasing the note with the fretting hand.

WIDE VIBRATO: The pitch is varied to a greater degree by vibrating with the fretting hand.

HAMMER-ON: Strike the first (lower) note with one finger, then sound the higher note (on the same string) with another finger by fretting it without picking.

PULL-OFF: Place both fingers on the notes to be sounded. Strike the first note and without picking, pull the finger off to sound the second (lower) note.

LEGATO SLIDE: Strike the first note and then slide the same fret-hand finger up or down to the second note. The second note is not struck.

SHIFT SLIDE: Same as legato slide, except the second note is struck.

TRILL: Very rapidly alternate between the notes indicated by continuously hammering on and pulling off.

TAPPING: Hammer ("tap") the fret indicated with the pick-hand index or middle finger and pull off to the note fretted by the fret hand.

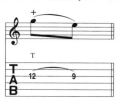

NATURAL HARMONIC: Strike the note while the fret-hand lightly touches the string directly over the fret indicated.

PINCH HARMONIC: The note is fretted normally and a harmonic is produced by adding the edge of the thumb or the tip of the index finger of the pick hand to the normal pick attack.

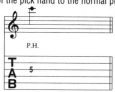

PICK SCRAPE: The edge of the pick is rubbed down (or up) the string, producing a scratchy sound.

MUFFLED STRINGS: A percussive sound is produced by laying the fret hand across the string(s) without depressing, and striking them with the pick hand.

PALM MUTING: The note is partially muted by the pick hand lightly touching the string(s) just before the bridge.

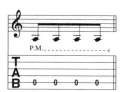

RAKE: Drag the pick across the strings indicated with a single motion.

TREMOLO PICKING: The note is picked as rapidly and continuously as possible.

VIBRATO BAR DIVE AND RETURN: The pitch of the note or chord is dropped a specified number of steps (in rhythm) then returned to the original pitch.

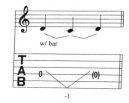

VIBRATO BAR SCOOP: Depress the bar just before striking the note, then quickly release the bar.

VIBRATO BAR DIP: Strike the note and then immediately drop a specified number of steps, then release back to the original pitch.

GUITAR *signature licks*

The Signature Licks book/audio packs are especially formatted to give you instruction on how to play a particular artist style by using the actual transcribed, "right from the record" licks! Designed for use by anyone from beginner right up to the experienced player who is looking to expand his insight. The books contain full performance notes and an overview of each artist or group's style with transcriptions in notes and tab. The audio features playing tips and techniques as well as playing examples at a slower tempo.

Acoustic Guitar Of '60s And '70s
by Wolf Marshall
A step-by-step breakdown of acoustic guitar styles and techniques featuring 14 classic rock examples, including: Here Comes The Sun • Fire And Rain • Dust In The Wind • Babe, I'm Gonna Leave You • Angie • and more.

00695024 Book/CD Pack......................$19.95

Acoustic Guitar Of '80s And '90s
by Wolf Marshall
Learn to play acoustic guitar in the styles and techniques of today's top performers. This book/CD pack features detailed instruction on 15 examples, including: Tears In Heaven • Patience • Losing My Religion • Wanted Dead Or Alive • and more.

00695033 Book/CD Pack......................$19.95

The Best Of Eric Clapton
by Jeff Perrin
A step-by-step breakdown of his playing technique through a hands-on analysis of classics. Includes: After Midnight • Crossroads • Layla • Tears In Heaven • Wonderful Tonight • and more.

00695038 Book/CD Pack......................$19.95

The Best Of Def Leppard
A step-by-step breakdown of the band's guitar styles and techniques featuring songs from four albums. The audio accompaniment presents each song in a stereo split with full band backing. Songs include: Bringin' On The Heartbreak • Hysteria • Photograph • and more.

00696516 Book/CD Pack......................$19.95

Jimi Hendrix
12 songs presented with all of the guitar parts fully transcribed, plus accompanying audio on CD, as performed by a full band. A performance notes, outlining chord voicings, scale use, and unusual techniques are including for each song. Songs include: Foxy Lady • Hey Joe • Little Wing • Purple Haze • and more.

00696560 Book/CD Pack......................$19.95

Eric Johnson
Learn the nuances of technique and taste that make Eric Johnson unique among guitarists. On this pack's 60-minute audio supplement, Wolf Marshall explores both the theoretical and hands-on aspects of Eric Johnson's best recorded work. It also comprehensively explores: Hybrid picking • String-skipping • Motivic development • Scale-combining • Position shifting • and additional aspects of his playing that makes him one of the most admired guitarists today. Some of his best songs are examined, including: Trademark • Cliffs Of Dover • Song For George • and more.
00699317 Book/CD Pack......................$19.95
00699318 Book/Cassette Pack..................$17.95

The Best Of Kiss
Learn the trademark riffs and solos behind one of rock's most legendary bands. This pack includes a hands-on analysis of 12 power house classics, including: Deuce • Strutter • Rock And Roll All Nite • Detroit Rock City • and more.

00699412 Book/Cassette Pack......................$17.95
00699413 Book/CD Pack......................$19.95

The Guitars Of Elvis
by Wolf Marshall
Elvis' music is synonymous with the birth of rock and roll and the invention of rock guitar. Wolf Marshall takes you back to the roots where it all started with this exploration into the influential style of the King's fretmen. This book is a step-by-step breakdown of the playing techniques of Scotty Moore, Hank Garland, and James Burton. Players will learn their unique concepts and techniques by studying this special collection of Elvis' greatest guitar-driven moments. The 75-minute accompanying audio presents each song in stereo-split with full band backing. Songs include: A Big Hunk O' Love • Heartbreak Hotel • Hound Dog • Jailhouse Rock • See See Rider • and more!
00696508 Book/Cassette Pack......................$17.95
00696507 Book/CD Pack......................$19.95

Rolling Stones
by Wolf Marshall
A step-by-step breakdown of the guitar styles of Keith Richards, Brian Jones, Mick Taylor and Ron Wood. 17 songs are explored, including: Beast Of Burden • It's Only Rock 'n' Roll (But I Like It) • Not Fade Away • Start Me Up • Tumbling Dice • and more.

00695079 Book/CD Pack......................$19.95

Best Of Carlos Santana
Explore the music behind one of the guitar's greatest innovators. A Hands-on analysis of 13 classics, including Black Magic Woman • Evil Ways • Oye Como Va • Song Of The Wind • and more.

00695010 Book/CD Pack......................$19.95

Steve Vai
Play along with the actual backing tracks from *Passion and Warfare* and *Sex and Religion* especially modified by Steve Vai himself! Learn the secrets behind a guitar virtuoso then play along like the pro himself.

00673247 Book/CD Pack......................$22.95

Stevie Ray Vaughan
by Wolf Marshall
This book takes you on an in-depth exploration of this guitar genius by examining various aspects of Vaughan's playing. Marshall explains his influences, tuning, equipment, picking technique and other aspects of Vaughan's sound. In addition, he transcribes, in notes and tab, parts of 13 of Vaughan's most famous songs, and explains how they were played and what makes them so unique. The 59-minute accompanying cassette or CD includes samples of the parts of the songs being examined. A must for any serious Vaughan fan or aspiring guitarist!
00699315 Book/Cassette Pack......................$17.95
00699316 Book/CD Pack......................$19.95

Prices, contents, and availability subject to change without notice. Some products may not be available outside the U.S.A.

FOR MORE INFORMATION, SEE YOUR LOCAL MUSIC DEALER,
OR WRITE TO:

HAL•LEONARD
CORPORATION
7777 W. BLUEMOUND RD. P.O. BOX 13819 MILWAUKEE, WI 53213
http://www.halleonard.com

0298